Pink Floyd
The Illustrated Biography

Pink Floyd
The Illustrated Biography

MARIE CLAYTON

**Trans
Atlantic
Press**

Published by Transatlantic Press
First published in 2010
This edition published 2012

Transatlantic Press
38 Copthorne Road
Croxley Green
Hertfordshire
WD3 4AQ

© Transatlantic Press
Photographs © see page 224

A catalogue record for this book is available
from the British Library.

ISBN 978-1-907176-55-5

Printed and bound in China

Contents

Introduction

Formed towards the end of the 1960s, Pink Floyd quickly became renowned for their progressive music and thoughtful lyrics, as well as for the psychedelic lighting effects and quadraphonic sound at their concerts. During the 1970s they released a series of concept albums, beginning with the phenomenally successful The Dark Side Of The Moon, which shot the group to instant superstardom when it was released in 1973. The following albums, Wish You Were Here, Animals and The Wall, confirmed Pink Floyd as one of rock music's most critically acclaimed and commercially successful bands.

During the 1970s and early 1980s the group's elaborate stage shows with their special effects were legendary, but by the mid-1980s guitarist and main lyricist Roger Waters had become disillusioned with playing the vast arenas that were necessary to accommodate their legions of fans. He decided to leave Pink Floyd, declaring that it was a "spent force", and for a while the future of the group hung in the balance. However, guitarist David Gilmour was determined to keep the band alive and, along with drummer Nick Mason and keyboard player Richard Wright, he took Pink Floyd to further worldwide success. After a gap of 20 years Waters and the other band members were reunited on stage at Live 8 London, for what turned out to be the last live performance featuring the classic Pink Floyd line up. Since then Richard Wright has died and the others are pursuing solo careers, but the legend of Pink Floyd lives on in their albums, most of which are re-released regularly and still sell in vast numbers.

Part One

The Piper at the Gates of Dawn

From Cambridge to London

Early publicity shot of Pink Floyd in the mid 1960s, from left: Roger Waters, Nick Mason, Syd Barrett, Richard Wright. Born Roger Keith Barrett in Cambridge in 1946, Syd had acquired his nickname when he was a teenager and became interested in music, since there was a well-known local musician named Sid Barrett. Roger Waters was born in Great Bookham in Surrey in 1943, but the following year his family moved to Cambridge, where he later became close friends with Syd. In the early sixties Syd was already a budding musician and member of a short-lived local band, Geoff Mott and the Mottoes, but Roger was planning to become an architect. In 1962, when he was 16, Syd won a two-year scholarship to study at Cambridge College of Arts and Technology and the same year, aged 19, Roger moved away from Cambridge to London to study architecture at Regent Street Polytechnic.

In London, Roger Waters became much more interested in music and invested some of his grant money in an acoustic guitar. Later he began living in a shared house with Nick Mason and Richard Wright, who were on the same college course, and the three of them joined a band formed by fellow students Clive Metcalf and Keith Noble, which was initially called Sigma 6, but later became The Abdabs, or sometimes The Screaming Abdabs. By 1964, The Abdabs had become the accepted "college" band, performing regularly at college dances. In 1964 Syd Barrett also arrived in London, to study art at Camberwell School of Art, and he soon hooked up with his old friend Roger.

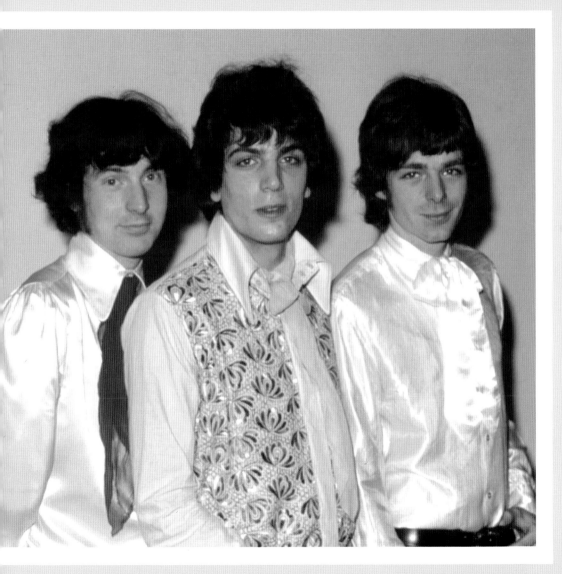

The Tea Set

As well as Syd Barrett another musician from the Cambridge scene, Rado "Bob" Klose, had come down to London and just after they arrived Nick Mason and Richard Wright moved out of the house they shared with Roger Waters so the newcomers were able to move in. Barrett, Waters, Mason and Klose soon formed a new band, and since their landlord Mike Leonard – a lecturer at the college they all attended – was a keen musician he was sometimes invited to join in. The line up had Syd Barrett on rhythm guitar, Roger Waters on bass guitar, Nick Mason on drums, Bob Klose on guitar, and Mike Leonard on keyboards. At first the new band was named Leonard's Lodgers, but later briefly became The Spectrum Five and then The Tea Set. It was reasonably successful, appearing at several concerts in colleges and small venues around London and at private parties. Richard Wright, meanwhile, had dropped out of his college course and headed off for an extended holiday abroad before starting a new course at the Royal College of Music.

October 1966: the first all-night rave

Pink Floyd on stage at the Roundhouse, Chalk Farm, London, on October 15, 1966 during the International Times All Night Rave. During 1965 both the name and the line up of the band had changed a few times; at first Bob Klose, Syd Barrett and Roger Waters all sang vocals, but later Chris Dennis – another Cambridge boy who was serving at the nearby Royal Air Force base at Uxbridge – was invited to join as lead singer. He left early in 1965 when he was posted abroad, leaving Barrett to take over as the main vocalist, and at around the same time Richard Wright returned to the UK and was quickly drafted in to replace Mike Leonard on keyboards. The band at this point was still called The Tea Set, but soon afterwards became Pink Floyd, apparently because there was another local band also called The Tea Set. The new name was coined on the spur of the moment by Barrett, and came from combining the names of two American musicians that he greatly admired: Pink Anderson and Floyd "Dipper Boy" Council.

Roger Waters performing onstage with Pink Floyd during a UFO concert at The Blarney Club in Tottenham Court Road, London, on December 23, 1966. During the remainder of 1965 the band had performed several times, sometimes billed as Pink Floyd and sometimes as The Tea Set, but by the beginning of 1966 had finally settled on the name Pink Floyd. Bob Klose left the band in mid-1965, leaving a final line up of Syd Barrett on rhythm guitar and vocals, Roger Waters on bass guitar and vocals, Nick Mason on drums and Richard Wright on keyboards, saxophone and vocals.

Lights, music, action

Pink Floyd on stage towards the end of 1966. The band had performed at a "psychodilia" music event staged at Hornsey College of Art in November 1966, and students at the college had designed a light show for the evening under the auspices of the band's old landlord, Mike Leonard, who was also a lecturer at Hornsey. Leonard had been developing a "light and sound" system in which the light effects were controlled by the sound, first using recorded and then live music. The use of coloured and moving lighting effects soon became an essential part of Pink Floyd's stage show, and one of the trademark features of their performance.

Roger Waters on his Rickenbacker 4001S bass guitar. Previously he had played lead guitar and then rhythm guitar, but when Bob Klose – an accomplished guitar player – joined the band, Roger switched to bass instead. At first the band's set list mainly consisted of rhythm and blues material from established artists such as Bo Diddley, Muddy Waters and Chuck Berry – like many other fledgling bands at the time – but they soon began to include more original material written by Syd Barrett. After Bob Klose left the band and Syd became front man, the direction changed to include more improvised and original music, with classical influences introduced by Richard Wright.

1966: A completed line up

The first stabilized line up of Pink Floyd in 1966, from left to right Roger Waters, Nick Mason, Syd Barrett and Richard Wright. The band had already tried recording a few numbers to send out as a promotional ploy to secure more live gigs, but it was a series of repeat performances at The Marquee Club in London during the first half of 1966 that really began to move their music career forward. These gigs were not so much concerts as performance events – albeit on a small scale – and although they were not widely advertised they found a key audience through word-of-mouth, and at one of these budding pop group manager Peter Jenner heard Pink Floyd play. Jenner had already been instrumental in getting a recording contract for avante garde group, AMM – also regulars at The Marquee Club – but he realized that this new band could be the more mainstream group he was looking for. At this stage, Pink Floyd were still playing mainly blues numbers, but were already beginning to improvise and include more abstract sounds within their set. Jenner's initial approach was rebuffed since the band members were all still full-time students and not sure if they were planning to continue playing, but when he approached them again later that year they agreed that he could represent them.

February 1967: Signed by EMI

Opposite: From left to right, Roger Waters, Nick Mason, Syd Barrett and Richard Wright. Having signed up Pink Floyd, Jenner brought a new partner into his business, his old friend Andrew King, who was in charge of booking gigs and also provided funding for new amplifiers. The company, called Blackhill Enterprises, had some success at booking the band for a series of concerts at small venues, and later that year forged a partnership with up-and-coming booking experts the Bryan Morrison Agency, who had established contacts with national venues. Pink Floyd had now begun to receive good coverage in the music press and soon began work on a demo tape to secure a recording deal, as well as recording soundtrack music for a documentary, *Tonite Let's All Make Love In London*, funded by the British Film Institute.

Above: Roger Waters in back projection during one of Pink Floyd's shows in 1967. Jenner's former partner, John Hopkins, had introduced the band to Americans Joel and Toni Brown, who created lighting effects using slide projections to enhance their act. Such effects had become common in America but caused a sensation in London, and news of these new and exciting performances spread like wildfire. Meanwhile Pink Floyd's demo tape was played to several major record companies, and by February 1 they were signed to EMI and the four band members had given up their studies for good and turned professional. Although the deal did not offer much money, it did allow them considerable creative freedom.

The first single

Opposite and above: Pink Floyd during rehearsals, left to right Nick Mason, Syd Barrett, Roger Waters. The band had recorded "Arnold Layne" – an original song written by Syd Barrett – in January 1967 as part of their demo tape, since it was a traditional pop song with catchy lyrics. EMI selected it to be the first single and had planned to re-record it in their own studio with their producer, but in the event it was the original demo recording that was released. The lyrics told the story of a transvestite who stole women's underwear from washing lines – which led some radio stations to refuse to play it, although it received plenty of airtime from the BBC. There was even a short film of the band on Wittering beach to promote the single, and they were recorded for BBC's *Top Of The Pops*, although the segment was never broadcast. The single reached the UK Top 20, but did not make it any further up the charts.

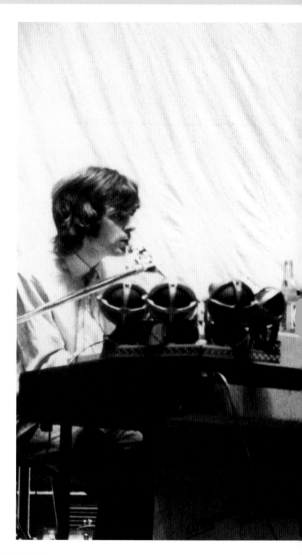

Games for May

Richard Wright, Nick Mason and Syd Barrett rehearsing for Pink Floyd's first concept show, Games for May, at the Queen Elizabeth Hall in London, on May 12, 1967. The show featured an early experiment with quadrophonic sound, with additional speakers placed at the back of the hall to create a primitive "surround-sound" effect, controlled by a joystick that could direct the sound from any point. It also had the by now trademark light-and-film display augmented by bubble machines, while during certain sections real flowers were tossed into the audience. Promoter Christopher Hunt had previously specialized in classical music, but he took a risk with Pink Floyd and this concert became a turning point in their career, firmly removing them from the underground music scene and into the mainstream. Several new compositions were written for the show, including "Games For May", which became the basis for the next single, "See Emily Play".

Meeting the Press

Above: EMI's new band meet the press outside EMI House. Left to right: Nick Mason, Rick Wright, Syd Barrett and Roger Waters (opposite: Roger Waters, Nick Mason, Syd Barrett and Rick Wright).

Reviews of Games for May were generally positive: the *International Times* hailed it as "a genuine 20th century chamber music concert", while the *Financial Times* called it "the noisiest and prettiest display ever seen on the South Bank". Unfortunately the bubbles and the flower petals stained the seat upholstery and carpet, and Pink Floyd were banned from ever playing the venue again. Worse still, the prototype sound control system – designed by Bernard Speight, an engineer in EMI's Abbey Road Studios, and dubbed the Azimuth Coordinator – was stolen after the show.

Top Of The Pops

Richard Wright, Syd Barrett and Roger Waters check out the timpani during rehearsals for Games For May. The second single, "See Emily Play", was released just after Games For May and did significantly better in the charts than the group's first attempt. As a result, in July they finally appeared on BBC television's flagship show *Top Of The Pops* and were featured for three weeks in a row.

Piper at the gates

Roger Waters, Syd Barrett, Nick Mason and Richard Wright in 1967, around the time of the release of their first album, *The Piper At The Gates Of Dawn*. Unusually for the period the deal with EMI had included the development of an album, although the contemporary market was mostly for singles. Although EMI were convinced that Pink Floyd were good, their music was very unlike that of other groups so a decision had been taken to allow them as much creative freedom as possible and see what ensued. The title of the LP came from the name of a chapter in *The Wind in the Willows*, by Kenneth Grahame, and the tracks included a mixture of songs and instrumentals. It was received very positively on release, and although it only reached No.6 in the UK albums chart it went on to become regarded as one of the seminal psychedelic albums of the sixties.

The cult of LSD

Clockwise from back left, Syd Barrett, Nick Mason, Richard Wright and Roger Waters. Photographer Andrew Whittuck invited the band to set up their gear in a bedroom of his parents' house in Hampstead, along with their light show, and took a series of atmospheric pictures. The light show used had been designed by Joe Gannon, a former Hornsey College of Art student, who was Pink Floyd's first full time touring technician and remained with them until late 1967. However, the whole concept of using psychedelic lighting effects was brought into question during the first half of 1967, after the British weekly *News Of The World* claimed that they were intended to illustrate the effect of certain hallucinogenic drugs, and that Pink Floyd's music celebrated drug abuse. The debate led to at least one concert being cancelled, and EMI quickly issued a statement denying that the music had any connection to drugs in any form. Pink Floyd themselves also went on record to state that to them the term "psychedelic" meant the use of sound and light as part of their performance and was not meant to promote the use of LSD or any other drug.

1967: Riots on the road

Roger Waters (left) photographed by Andrew Whittuck with psychedelic light effects, and clockwise from back left (opposite), Syd Barrett, Nick Mason, Richard Wright, Roger Waters. Although Pink Floyd had found an audience in London, out of the capital it was a very different story. Many of those coming to concerts in the provinces had turned up expecting to hear music similar to the band's singles, and were usually outraged to be presented instead with a wave of indeterminate noise played at very high volume and long instrumentals lasting ten minutes or more. They lost little time in making their displeasure known, throwing beer glasses, shouting torrents of abuse or simply walking out. It wasn't long before promoters began to insist that the band signed a clause to ensure they would at least play their released songs as part of their set – although Pink Floyd never gave up on their determination to introduce more avant-garde material as well.

Problems escalate

Syd Barrett, photographed by Andrew Whittuck with psychedelic light effects. Although he was a supremely talented songwriter and a charismatic personality, Syd didn't have the natural enthusiasm and extrovert personality required for being constantly in the limelight and found the pressure very difficult to handle. Most members of Pink Floyd had nothing to do with drugs during this period, but Syd had begun to experiment heavily with LSD and instead of helping him relax it often brought on bouts of severe stage fright. From mid-1967 onwards his behaviour became increasingly unpredictable and this soon began to cause problems in Pink Floyd's professional life. At some performances he would just stand still, not playing or singing, and at an important recording session for the BBC he freaked out and the session had to be abandoned. In an attempt to resolve the situation, that August Pink Floyd's managers Blackhill announced that Syd was suffering from nervous exhaustion and cancelled all concerts for the rest of the month.

September 1967:
A European tour

Pink Floyd in Copenhagen, Denmark, during their first overseas tour. In September 1967, Pink Floyd headed off to Europe on a tour that began in Äarhus, Denmark, and visited Stockholm in Sweden, and finished with three concerts in Copenhagen, Denmark. It was during this tour that Roger Waters began to take over as the main spokesman for the band, since Syd was sometimes not in a fit state to be interviewed. From Copenhagen the band headed straight over to Ireland, where they played concerts in Belfast, Ballymena and Cork. On their return to the UK there was no let up – they moved immediately into a hectic series of concerts over the remainder of the month.

In the recording studio

Roger Waters (opposite) at the microphone in the recording studio and with Nick Mason, Syd Barrett and Richard Wright (above) at a mixing desk in the recording studio control room. Although they had not played any concerts in August the band had not neglected their recording commitments, spending time in the studio putting together tracks for their planned next album. In October they returned to the studio for more sessions, and to record the next single, "Apples and Oranges".

The first album had mainly been filled with Barrett compositions, but he had provided very little new material for this new one so both Roger Waters and Richard Wright stepped into the breach to come up with a selection of tracks between them. "Apples and Oranges" was the last Barrett composition to be released as a Pink Floyd single, but it did not do as well in the charts as their previous singles.

November 1967: First tour of the United States

Above: Roger Waters, Nick Mason, Syd Barrett and Richard Wright around the time of their first US tour in 1967. Pink Floyd's first tour to the States had originally been timed to coincide with the release of their first album there at the end of October, but problems in getting the visas sorted out in time had meant that the first few dates had to be cancelled. On top of this, the band's celebrated light show did not look at all spectacular in the massive American venues, although the slide projections were still acceptable. And apart from the technical problems, it was on this tour that Syd Barrett really began to fall apart, sometimes standing stock still without playing or detuning his guitar until the strings fell off during concerts, and refusing to answer questions when interviewed. It wasn't long before Pink Floyd were packed off back to the UK, with several important gigs cancelled.

Opposite: Syd Barrett in the recording studio.

A change of direction

Above: Nick Mason, Syd Barrett, Richard Wright and Roger
Waters relaxing between takes in the studio. By the end of 1967
Pink Floyd had begun to change direction. It was not only that
the age of Flower Power was beginning to come to an end –
Syd could apparently no longer write the catchy, poetical songs
the band had relied on and new material by Roger Waters was
darker and more intense. Perhaps realizing that his days were
numbered – or perhaps just under the influence of drugs – Syd

was creating as much havoc in private as he had on stage,
taunting the others with a new song that could not be learnt
because it changed on every take, or insisting that they should
add a female vocalist or a saxophone player to the line up.
Word soon began to circulate that Pink Floyd were looking for
an "additional" guitarist to join them.

Opposite: Roger Waters with acoustic guitar in the studio.

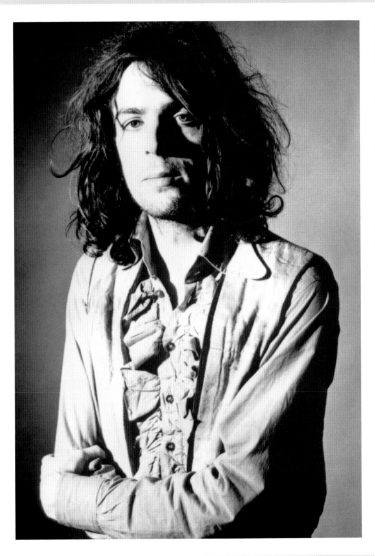

The end of the beginning

Opposite: Richard Wright, Nick Mason, Roger Waters and Syd Barrett. The original plan was to have a guitarist on hand who could cover for Syd (right) when he was not functioning, and would otherwise act as a back up player. The ideal person seemed to be David Gilmour, who had been a friend of Syd's back in Cambridge and who was a talented guitarist. Gilmour had enjoyed some success with previous bands but opportunities had ended up coming to nothing so he accepted Pink Floyd's offer immediately. He learned Syd's vocal and guitar parts, but almost immediately it became apparent that the plan was not going to work. The five-man Pink Floyd played a few concerts in January 1969, but Syd did less and less each time until finally the others just didn't bother to pick him up one day on the way to a gig.

Barrett's departure

Syd Barrett, Richard Wright, Nick Mason and Roger Waters photographed in London. The departure of Barrett left deep scars; each of the others – even David Gilmour, who had replaced him – had been friends with Syd for years and they felt they had betrayed him in some way. However, his mental and physical disintegration had not only been painful for them to watch and impossible to cope with, but had also come close to destroying Pink Floyd. At first they thought perhaps he could just continue to write songs and not perform, but even this did not work. Another consequence of the upheaval was a change in their management; Peter Jenner and Andrew King of Blackhill Enterprises were convinced that Syd was the creative genius behind the band and that without him Pink Floyd had no future. They chose to dissolve their partnership with the group but to continue with Syd as a solo artist and the Bryan Morrison Agency, with whom Pink Floyd already had a good working relationship, took over the band's new management.

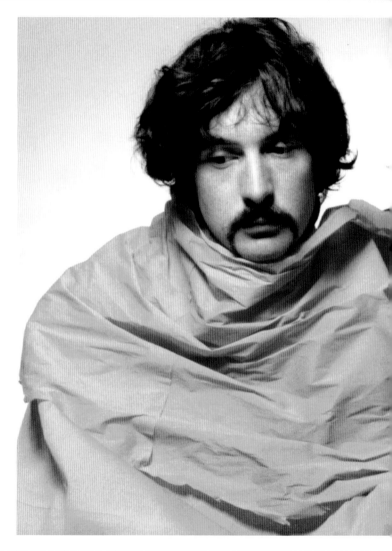

A new line up

The new Pink Floyd – from left to right Nick Mason, David Gilmour, Roger Waters, with Richard Wright at the front. David Gilmour said later that he found it difficult to take his place as a full member of the band at first, partly because of the shadow of Syd over all of them, and partly because there was no clear idea of the role he should be playing. Although he was undoubtedly talented, his natural style was very different to Syd's so it was not just a question of stepping straight into empty shoes. Of the other three, Richard Wright was the most accomplished musician, while Roger Waters and Nick Mason – although not as good musicians technically – had a vision of what they wanted Pink Floyd to be and how their music should be presented. The next album, *A Saucerful Of Secrets*, released in June 1968, was a reflection of this time of flux – it had no real sense of direction, except that it had moved away from psychedelia. Despite this, it was quite well received.

Conquering Europe and the USA

Above: David Gilmour, Roger Waters, Nick Mason and Richard Wright photographed towards the end of 1969. During the remainder of 1968, Pink Floyd carried out a couple of short tours round Europe and also played at a couple of festivals in Italy and The Netherlands, which firmly consolidated their position overseas. Syd had not really made much of an impression as the front man in Europe, so the change of line up made very little difference to the fans. There was also another short tour of North America that once again was affected by the late arrival of visas, leading to cancelled concerts and hastily arranged alternative venues. However, despite the chaos surrounding the arrangements, the tour did bring Pink Floyd a fervent crowd of North American fans and excellent reviews in the press. There was also another change of management: the Bryan Morrison Agency was sold to NEMS in mid-1968, but since Pink Floyd had never signed a formal management contract after transferring from Blackhill they were able to opt out from the sale. Instead Steve O'Rourke – who had looked after the band on behalf of Bryan Morrison – was released from joining NEMS and became their personal manager.

Opposite: Richard Wright at the keyboards.

Moon landing

David Gilmour on stage. In June 1968 Blackhill Enterprises staged the first free concert in Hyde Park, and Pink Floyd were invited to headline the event. It was the ideal opportunity to re-launch the band in the UK and unveil the new direction their music was taking, and their performance firmly established them as a major talent in the UK music scene, both with the press and the fans. During 1969, Pink Floyd consolidated their position in the UK with a spectacular event at the Royal Festival Hall that featured the new Azimuth Coordinator, a 360° surround sound system, and the music arranged to tell a story so the performance became more theatrical event than concert. By this period fans did not expect to dance to Pink Floyd music – it was designed to be listened to and enjoyed. 1969 also saw Pink Floyd embarking on their first proper national tour of the UK, headlining at such major venues as Fairfield Halls in Croydon and the Royal Philharmonic in Liverpool, and culminating in a stupendous concert at the Royal Albert Hall in London. They also recorded the soundtrack for the movie *More*, and released their own new album, *Ummagumma*, but perhaps the highlight of the year was an invitation to compose the music for the BBC's coverage of the Apollo 11 moon landing, which was broadcast to millions of viewers and brought the band amazing publicity.

Part Two

Atom Heart Mother

1970: A No.1 hit

Nick Mason on stage in Copenhagen, Denmark, on November 12, 1970. At the beginning of 1970 the eagerly awaited new film by Antonioni was released, featuring music by Pink Floyd. *Zabriskie Point*, about student rebellion, was originally to have a complete score by Pink Floyd, but the director finally settled for just three pieces. Despite this, the film brought the band even more positive exposure – particularly in the US – and on the back of all the heightened interest two new tours of North America were arranged, as well as another tour of Europe. In between their concert commitments the band had also gone back to the studio to develop an instrumental piece that would become the basis of the next album, *Atom Heart Mother*.

David Gilmour in Denmark, in 1970. The new instrumental featured an orchestra and a choir and took up the whole of one side of the album. On the other side each band member is featured in an individual track – an idea that had also been explored in Pink Floyd's previous album, *Ummagumma*. "If" was written and sung by Roger Waters, "Summer '68" was written and performed by Richard Wright, "Fat Old Sun" was written and performed by David Gilmour, and "Alan's Psychedelic Breakfast", an instrumental in three parts divided by dialogue and sound effects of one of the roadies preparing breakfast in Nick Mason's kitchen, had sound effects created mainly by Mason. Although in later years both Waters and Gilmour were very critical of *Atom Heart Mother*, when it was released it brought the band their first No.1, in the UK Album Chart.

A series of tours

David Gilmour, Nick Mason, Roger Waters and Richard Wright on stage in Copenhagen, Denmark, during 1970. The title of *Atom Heart Mother* came about in a typically Pink Floyd random fashion: the instrumental had been called "The Amazing Pudding" as a working title but the band knew they needed something better. While discussing the matter with music journalist John Peel and composer Ron Geesin – who had helped in the development of the orchestral section –

Geesin picked up Peel's copy of the *Evening Standard* newspaper and handed it to Roger Waters, suggesting that he would find a title inside. Waters opened the paper at random and read out "Atom Heart Mother" and the others instantly agreed that this was perfect. The words were part of a headline about a mother who had just received the first plutonium-based pacemaker.

David Gilmour and Nick Mason. Pink Floyd managed to pack in two tours of Europe, several festivals in France and two tours of North America in 1970, as well as a whole series of concerts across the UK. Plans were also put in place to take *Atom Heart Mother* out on tour at the end of the year, although the logistics of travelling with an orchestra and a choir proved very difficult – not to mention recreating the kitchen sequence for "Alan's Psychedelic Breakfast". Meanwhile renowned movie director Stanley Kubrick had approached the band for permission to use the title track from *Atom Heart Mother* in the film he was making, *A Clockwork Orange*. Initially the band were interested, but Kubrick had no idea how he would use the music and wanted a free hand to do as he pleased so in the end the band turned him down.

Bath Festival of Blues & Progressive Music '70

David Gilmour performing live in 1970. The music festival at Bath in Somerset was a three-day event, the forerunner to Glastonbury, and it was here that Pink Floyd unveiled "Atom Heart Mother" officially for the first time, with a live orchestra and choir on stage. The festival, which featured some of the world's best groups, had an audience of around 150,000 and Pink Floyd did not come onto the stage until very early on Sunday morning when most festival-goers had been up all night. However, their spectacular performance woke everyone up; they not only performed "Atom Heart Mother" – which had not yet been released – but also some of their older classics such as "Careful With That Axe, Eugene" and "Set The Controls For The Heart Of The Sun".

Roger Waters takes a turn on the drums. The day after the Bath festival, Pink Floyd appeared at The Holland Pop Festival in Rotterdam, The Netherlands, which was the biggest event of its kind in the area. They performed "Atom Heart Mother" again, but this time managed without the live orchestra. The orchestra was also proving a problem in the recording studio, as the musicians had a tendency to vanish to the canteen whenever proceedings paused and Geesin – who was not a trained conductor – found it very difficult to keep them on track. Eventually John Aldiss, director of the choir, stepped in as conductor and kept them all in line. Pink Floyd soon realized that a trained conductor would be an essential part of any live performance of the work.

July 1970: Hyde Park

Left and opposite: David Gilmour performing live during the 1970s. In July 1970 Blackhill Enterprises organized their third Hyde Park concert and Pink Floyd were invited to headline the show for a second time. They performed "Atom Heart Mother" again with an orchestra and choir, as well as staples such as "Careful With That Axe, Eugene" and "Set The Controls For The Heart Of The Sun". A review in *Disc & Music Echo* said, "The Pink Floyd gave an hour of beautifully mature music, soothing and inspiring to listen to."

August 1970: Summer in St Tropez

Roger Waters and David Gilmour. From the end of July and through into August, Pink Floyd and their entourage decamped to a villa in St Tropez, in the South of France. It was partly intended to be a holiday, but St Tropez was also a more convenient base to enable the group to appear at a series of music festivals that were planned to take place around the French Riviera that summer. Unfortunately several of these never materialized, or were cut short or cancelled due to rioting amongst the audience. In the end, Pink Floyd only appeared at the XI Festival International de Jazz in Juan les Pins, near Antibes, the Festival de St Tropez in St Tropez, and the Fête de St Raphaël at the Roman amphitheatre in Fréjus.

Two new albums

Richard Wright with his wife Juliette Gale, who he married in 1964 while they were both still at college. Juliette had performed with an early incarnation of Pink Floyd – she was vocalist with The Abdabs in 1964. The two divorced in 1982. After the success of *Atom Heart Mother*, the pressure was on to come up with another hit album as soon as possible. However, the band had tight touring schedules already in place so would not be able to spend a great deal of time in the recording studio for some time. As a temporary solution, EMI decided to put together a collection of songs from the early years – including "Arnold Layne" and "See Emily Play", from when Syd Barrett was with the band – that had either only been released as singles before, or been included on an album in a shorter version. It also included one previously unreleased track, "Biding My Time", by Roger Waters. This new album, entitled *Relics – A collection of Bizarre Antiques and Curios*, was a budget release so was not eligible for inclusion in the album charts, but it sold well and kept the eager fans happy until the band could come up with some new material.

Fans watching Pink Floyd in concert during the 1970s. By this time nobody came to see the Floyd in action and expected to dance along – instead it was more usual for the audience to listen in rapt attention. As David Gilmour commented later, "... in the quiet passages, you could hear a pin drop". Meanwhile the band had begun work on a new project: taking many unconnected bits of music, using ideas from previous sessions and working the whole lot together into a cohesive whole. This became a piece known as "Return Of The Son of Nothing", which was later renamed "Echos" and used as the entire first side of the next album, *Meddle*.

Playing live at Pompeii

David Gilmour in the early 1970s. In was in 1971 that Pink Floyd made their first tour to Japan and Australia. They appeared at two festivals and one concert in Japan, and at one evening and one afternoon concert in Australia. They also handled their most extensive North American tour to date, over ten states plus three venues in Canada. However, the highlight of the year was a collaboration with French film director Adrian Maben, who as the heart of his documentary filmed them performing against the dramatic backdrop of the ancient Roman amphitheatre at Pompeii. The film also included candid interviews, live sequences – and the first performance of "Speak To Me", which was to become the opening sequence of the next album, *Dark Side of The Moon*. The resulting documentary, *Pink Floyd Live At Pompeii*, received rave reviews at the Edinburgh Film Festival the following year, although it didn't go on general release until two years later.

Roger Waters backstage at the Olympisch Stadion in Amsterdam in May 1972. During 1971 Pink Floyd had done four major overseas tours, as well as countless concerts around the UK, and a documentary film of their performance. The set list for most of these events had concentrated on much the same material, so now there was a real sense that they needed to come up with something fresh and new – ideally in time for the next tour, due to start at the end of January 1972. The material to fill half a concert would also be the right amount to fill a new album – and the other half of the concert could be used to play established favourites. Roger Waters came up with the concept of basing a series of pieces around one theme of madness: things that drove people mad, conflict, greed, the pressures of fame and success, the strains of touring away from home, fear of flying ... and mental breakdown, inspired by the memory of Syd Barrett.

1972: Development of *The Dark Side Of The Moon*

Richard Wright on stage in Copenhagen in 1972. Roger Waters had started writing lyrics for the new work at the end of 1971, and in the first few weeks of 1972 the band began rehearsing before taking the entire work on tour. They had often previewed individual pieces in concert before recording them, but this time they played the entire work, in the order it would later appear on the album, which gave them the opportunity to adjust and refine parts that needed improvement. They had already come up with the title The *Dark Side Of The Moon*, but unfortunately another band had recently released their album with the same name. For a while the Pink Floyd work was renamed "Eclipse", but the rival album did not do well, so by the time they were ready to release Pink Floyd were able to revert to their original title. It was at the first concert on a UK tour, at the Brighton Dome on January 20, 1972, that *The Dark Side Of The Moon* was to be played for the first time in its entirety but unfortunately technical problems led to only part being covered before the band moved on to other material. It was finally fully presented in mid-February, to immediate acclaim from both the musical and the national press. Opposite: Nick Mason onstage in Denmark in November 1972.

Obscured by Clouds

Richard Wright onstage in Copenhagen in 1972. Before Pink Floyd could begin recording *The Dark Side Of The Moon* they were invited to write the music soundtrack for a movie by French director Barbet Schroeder. The film, about a young woman's spiritual awakening, was set in New Guinea and titled *La Vallée* but the soundtrack album was released in June as *Obscured By Clouds* – although some copies featured the English title of the film, *The Valley*. The schedule for creating and recording the music was tight – only two weeks – and the band travelled to France to work on it there. They were based at Strawberry Studios at the Chateau d'Hérouville near Paris, where Elton John recorded *Honky Château* and David Bowie his album *Pinups*.

David Gilmour onstage in Copenhagen in 1972. Immediately after completing the main recording for *Obscured By Clouds* the Floyd were off again on a week-long tour of Japan. Only ten days after their return they were back at the studio outside Paris to finish off the new album. On its release, in June 1972, *Obscured By Clouds* reached No.6 in the UK Albums chart, but only managed No.49 in the Billboard Pop Albums chart. Two tracks from the album were released as a single; the band had pretty much given up on singles because none of the ones previously released had done that well and they had come to consider them too much trouble. For two years – 1969 and 1970 – they had released none at all; in 1971 there was only "One Of These Days" *from Meddle*, and now "Free Four" from this new album.

Back in the USA

Opposite: David Gilmour, Nick Mason and Roger Waters onstage in Denmark in November 1972. From mid-April to the beginning of May, Pink Floyd were touring North America, playing bigger venues than on their last visit but still managing to sell out tickets for most dates. Throughout the whole of 1972 they featured *The Dark Side Of The Moon* during the first half of almost all their concerts but played the more established material in the second half.

Right: Roger Waters onstage in Copenhagen, Denmark in November 1972. Writing all the lyrics for *The Dark Side Of The Moon* and managing to create a complete piece of work on one theme had given Roger Waters a new confidence in his abilities, and it was around this period that be began to consider himself as the main creative and driving force of Pink Floyd. However, there was as yet no sign of the disagreements that would ultimately tear the band apart.

November 1972: On to Europe

Opposite: Nick Mason onstage in Copenhagen, Denmark in November 1972. Mason has played the drums on all Pink Floyd's albums – but not on every song – and although he can play guitar and keyboards he has rarely played any other instrument on stage or in the recording studio. In August 1972 all members of the Floyd took the month off, but came back ready to hit America again at the beginning of September. This second US tour was only a month long and on their return it was back to the studio again to continue recording *The Dark Side Of The Moon*.

Right: David Gilmour onstage in Copenhagen, Denmark, in November 1972. An accomplished guitarist, he also plays the banjo, keyboards, drums and harmonica.

Hamburg 1972
Richard Wright, David Gilmour
and Nick Mason relaxing in
Hamburg in November 1972.
Most of the last two months of
1972 was taken up with an
extensive tour of northern
Europe, which covered
Denmark, West Germany,
France, Belgium, and
Switzerland. However, before
setting out for Europe Pink
Floyd played at a benefit
concert at Wembley, on behalf
of War On Want, The Albany
Trust Deptford and Save The
Children. A review of this in
Sounds said, "... a faultless
demonstration of what
psychedelic music is all about
... smoke mingled with the
coloured lights and the dry ice
surface mist to effectively whisk
us all away to Planet Floyd."

Richard Wright, David Gilmour, Nick Mason, Roger Waters in England 1973. Much of the first half of 1973 was taken up with a major US tour, the first leg of which covered twelve states, along with two dates in Canada, and ran throughout March to coincide with the release of *The Dark Side Of The Moon* album. A further eight more states were played during the second leg of the tour in June. It was all a far cry from the early days when Pink Floyd would arrive in a single van; now the tour equipment took up two 40-foot articulated trucks and the band travelled with their own stage hands, soundmen, electricians, lighting men and other technicians. The stage setting took nearly a full day to assemble at the venue; Richard Wright commented at the time, "Sometimes I look at our huge truck and tons of equipment and think, 'Christ, all I'm doing is playing an organ'."

1973: Birth of a supergroup

Opposite: Pink Floyd performing live onstage at a Shelter benefit concert in May during the Dark Side Of The Moon tour. After the album of The Dark Side Of The Moon was finally released in March 1973 it went straight to No.1 in the US Billboard 200 chart, had been certified Gold within less than a year and went on to become one of the best selling albums of all time. It is frequently ranked as one of the greatest rock albums of all time and its incredible success quickly propelled Pink Floyd to superstar status. Although in some respects this opened up new opportunities there was also a downside: as in the early days, many of the new fans coming to concerts were expecting to hear a similar kind of music that they could interact with and didn't want to sit and listen quietly like the hard-core Pink Floyd fans.

Above: Pink Floyd at the LA Sports Arena in 1973. The phenomenal selling power of The Dark Side Of The Moon album brought the members of the band considerable wealth for the first time and it was also at this time that their collaboration as a group was at its peak. Roger Waters later commented, "We had gelled as a group, we were working very well together ... it was very jolly. A wonderful time." However, the amazing success of the album was a surprise to them; as Nick Mason later said, "... everyone thought it was the best thing we'd ever done to date, and everyone was very pleased with it, but there's no way that anyone felt it was five times as good as *Meddle*, or eight times as good as *Atom Heart Mother*, or the sort of figures that it has in fact sold."

May 1973: Money, it's a crime

Opposite: Pink Floyd on stage in 1973. The song "Money" from *The Dark Side of the Moon* was released as a single in May 1973 and became the first Pink Floyd single to make it into the top twenty on the Billboard Hot 100 chart, peaking at No.13. It became one of the most popular Pink Floyd songs and was played in as part of the set list or as the encore for most concerts throughout the seventies. The music and lyrics were both written by Roger Waters, but the instrumental jam section was a group effort, with David Gilmour contributing guitar and vocals and Richard Wright and Nick Mason improvising their parts. In 2008 Gilmour's extended guitar solo in "Money" was voted No.62 in a poll of *Guitar World* readers to find the Greatest 100 Guitar Solos.

Above: David Gilmour, Nick Mason, Roger Waters and Richard Wright on stage in 1973. During the second half of 1973 Pink Floyd began working on their next album. Their initial idea was based on one of the elements from "Alan's Psychedelic Breakfast": they would make an entire album using ordinary household objects – with no musical instruments at all. They began recording in October that year with lots of ideas as to how this would work, but it soon became obvious that the effects produced were interesting but could not really be called music. Some of the ideas from the aborted "Household Objects" sessions – as they came to be called – were used in later albums, but the concept as a whole was dropped.

The Great Gig In The Sky

Left: Portrait of Richard Wright in the mid-1970s. Wright had co-written many of the tracks on *The Dark Side Of The Moon*, including "Breathe", "Time", "Us And Them" and "Any Colour You Like", and had also contributed lead vocals, with David Gilmour, to "Time" and "Us And Them". However, his most significant contribution to the album was the emotive and piano-led "The Great Gig in the Sky", which became one of the most popular tracks. Session singer and songwriter Clare Torry was invited to sing on the album but told there were no lyrics so she improvised a wordless melody to go with Wright's music.

Opposite: Pink Floyd on stage during The Dark Side Of The Moon tour in 1973. In November 1973 Pink Floyd teamed up with Soft Machine to play a benefit concert for recently disabled drummer Robert Wyatt – a founding member of Soft Machine – at the Rainbow Theatre in London. Music newspaper *Melody Maker* described the performance: "Clocks ticked mysteriously and with perfect precision the Floydmen slotted their live instruments into the recorded sound, combining quadraphonic pre-recorded tapes, lights, smoke and theatrical effects into a kind of rock Son et Lumière."

1974: New ideas

Left: David Gilmour, during a performance with singer Roy Harper at Hyde Park in 1974. At the end of 1973 the band decided they could afford to take some time off and there were no more concerts between November 4 and June 18. However, David Gilmour took the opportunity to become involved with other projects, helping to launch the career of singer/songwriter Kate Bush and new group Unicorn. Nick Mason also began to develop interests outside Pink Floyd, performing several times with fellow drummer Robert Wyatt.

Opposite: Pink Floyd playing soccer in Dijon, France on June 22, 1974 – when they arrived in Paris the band were also challenged to a game by French journalists, who beat them 4–3. Their tour of France had begun on June 18 in Toulouse and finished just over a week later with three nights in Paris. There were originally many more dates scheduled, but some venues realized they could not cope with the massive power requirements of the band's equipment, or did not have the ceiling height to accommodate the huge 40-foot circular back projection screen that now formed the backdrop to the stage set.

June 1974: On stage in France

Pink Floyd on stage in Dijon, France, on June 22. The huge circular screen at the back of the stage was used to display film and animation sequences during the show. Despite their resolve to take some time off the Floyd had not been idle before the start of the French tour; they had already been back into the recording studio to begin work on material for their next album. In addition they had re-released their first two albums as *A Nice Pair*, and in the US only they had released a single, "Time", taken from *The Dark Side of The Moon*.

Meanwhile Pink Floyd had broken with their US record company, Capitol Records, and had negotiated a new contract with Columbia Records – with a reported advance of a million dollars. Although Capitol had steadily released Pink Floyd singles over the years in the US and had really got behind promotion of *The Dark Side Of The Moon*, the band felt that overall they had not been well represented and that Capitol had often promoted other artists above them. It was also felt that the smaller company did not have the resources to take things forward in the future. However, in Europe the Floyd were still represented by Harvest Records, part of the EMI group.

Pink Floyd performing on stage – after the large circular screen made its appearance in 1974, it went on to become a trademark feature of the band's shows for some time. A film sequence produced to illustrate "Time" featured flying clock faces moving in time to the music, while "Money" had piles of silver coins. At the end of the show the circular screen formed the backdrop for an enormous mirror ball, which spun around throwing off reflected rays of brilliant light. During the course of this spectacular effect, the band would quietly leave the stage.

Portrait of drummer Nick Mason during the mid-1970s. Mason used his newfound wealth to indulge his interest in classic and upmarket cars – in fact, in an interview in the *Sunday Times* in 2004, he said that his first love had been cars rather than music. "The cars came first. My dad used to race a vintage Bentley and from my earliest memory, cars and racing were part of my life. I went to watch him at Silverstone in the early 1950s and I've still got the car he was in." Mason's car collection became so big that it had to be kept in hangars; 25–30 cars in the collection were racing cars of the very highest quality, spanning all eras from the turn of the century.

1974 British Winter Tour

Opposite: Nick Mason and Roger Waters performing live onstage on the 1974 British Winter Tour. Since the band were all big football fans, many of the dates on the tour were booked to coincide with major football games in each city. As usual, the concerts were used to preview and adjust some of the songs intended for the new album: "Shine On You Crazy Diamond", Raving and Drooling" and "Gotta Be Crazy". The second half of the concert covered *The Dark Side Of The Moon*, featuring stunning and innovative specially commissioned animation by Ian Eames.

Above: Richard Wright at the keyboards. Although the UK tour was a complete success with every venue sold out, some parts of the music press had begun to turn against Pink Floyd. In particular, young reviewer Nick Kent had been very dismissive of the band's new material in an article in *New Musical Express*. However, touring commitments meant further recording of the new album had to be put back to 1975 and fitted in between two US tours, so there was plenty of time to develop the material further.

Backstage in Birmingham

Back stage in the dressing room at the Hippodrome, Birmingham, on December 4, 1974, with Steve O'Rourke (opposite), who had been the Floyd's manager since 1968. By the time they reached Birmingham the band were becoming tired and jaded after nearly two months of almost constant touring and performing, but there was only a short break over Christmas and the New Year before they were scheduled to begin recording again for the next album, *Wish You Were Here*. Recording sessions were held at EMI's Abbey Road Studios from January 6 to March 3, 1975, but at the end the album was still nowhere near completed. By this time it had been nearly two years since Pink Floyd had released a new album – *A Nice Pair* was simply a re-release of the first two albums – and the record companies were pushing for something to sell. Sensing an opportunity, the band's old company, Capitol Records, released a compilation album, *Tour '75*, to satisfy the fans and build sales of the back catalogue that they still owned.

Touring North America

David Gilmour (left) and Richard
Wright (opposite) in Los Angeles,
California, in April 1975. Ticket sales
for all the US shows on the first tour
in 1975 had sold out within hours of
the dates being announced – the
Los Angeles venue sold all 67,000 of
its tickets in just one day. The scale
of the tour was vast and the logistics
mind-boggling: over 30 tons of
equipment was transported in a
convoy of articulated trucks, with a
road crew of seventeen in
attendance. On the west coast, in
mainly indoor arenas, the Pink Floyd
special effects still reigned supreme,
but on the east coast it was a
different story. Here they were
appearing in vast outdoor sports
arenas to accommodate their
legions of fans – and their staging
just wasn't up to it, looking small
and lost in such enormous spaces.
To remedy the situation, the Floyd
commissioned architectural
designers Mark Fisher and Jonathan
Park to design a large inflatable
pyramid to float above them during
the show. The idea was that it would
radiate light beams, thus appearing
like a huge representation of the
prism on the front of *The Dark Side
Of The Moon*.

June 1975: A visit from Syd

Left and opposite: David Gilmour on stage during 1975. During one of Pink Floyd's recording sessions at EMI's Abbey Road Studios for *Wish You Were Here*, Syd Barrett turned up at the studio to watch. None of the band recognized their former friend at first: he had put on quite a lot of weight, and had shaved off all his head hair, including his eyebrows. When Roger Waters realized who it was he became visibly upset, to the point of tears. According to legend, at the time of Syd's visit the band were listening to a final playback of "Shine On You Crazy Diamond", which had been written by Waters as a tribute to him – but both David Gilmour and Nick Mason later said they could not recall which particular song they were working on that day. It was the last time the members of the group were to see Syd: after suffering from diabetes for some time, he later developed pancreatic cancer and died at home in Cambridge in July 2006.

July 1975: Knebworth

Two days after Pink Floyd came back from the second leg of their US tour they were due to appear at a big open air concert at Knebworth Park, their first UK concert for seven months. The fans had been awaiting the event with great excitement, and the maximum licensed audience of 40,000 swelled to nearer 100,000 after perimeter fencing had to be removed because of the vast number of people who turned up. Unfortunately the waiting multitude did not get the fantastic performance they had expected; both the road crew and the band were still jet lagged from their recent transatlantic flight, and neither the staging nor their playing was at its best. In addition there were a host of technical problems: the planned flyby of two Second World War Spitfires at the start of their set arrived too early, the Floyd's own PA system – which had also been used by previous groups – partly failed due to insufficient generator power, and the mains power was at the wrong frequency, knocking the electric organ out of tune.

September 1975: Wish you were here?

By the latter half of 1975 the record company were really pushing for a new album to release. Pink Floyd had been working on *Wish You Were Here* off and on since January 1974, but without much enthusiasm. Roger Waters later said, "I definitely think that at the *Wish You Were Here* recording sessions, most of us didn't wish we were there at all, we wished we were somewhere else ... The album is about none of us really being there ... about our non-presence in the situation we had clung to through habit, and are still clinging to through habit: being Pink Floyd." The album changed direction during the recording; at Roger's suggestion they dropped two of the intended songs, "Raving and Drooling" and "Gotta Be Crazy", and split "Shine On You Crazy Diamond" into two halves, to start and finish the album. New songs were written to link the two halves: "Welcome To The Machine", "Wish You Were Here" and "Have A Cigar". Despite the problems during its creation, both Roger Waters and David Gilmour have each said that it is their favourite Pink Floyd album. It went straight to No.1 in the UK chart and reached the top spot in the US a week later, and has continued to sell well over the years: it was certified six times platinum (6 million copies sold) in May 1997.

Roger Waters (left) sang vocals on all the sections of "Shine On You Crazy Diamond" and had also planned to sing on "Have A Cigar", but unfortunately by the time they came to record that track his voice was suffering badly from strain. Luckily a close associate of the band, singer Roy Harper, was recording in an adjacent studio and he was asked to take over. Harper's version was used on a final album, but Waters always regretted that he was not able to do the song himself. David Gilmour (right) married his first wife, American-born Ginger, during recording of *Wish You Were Here*. The two of them went on to have four children, but divorced in 1990.

Animals tour

The Animals tour began in West Germany two days after the album was released and was built around performing both Animals and Wish You Were Here. During "Pigs" a giant inflatable pig was supposed to float around the stage above Pink Floyd, wreathed in billowing clouds of smoke – but it took a few attempts to get the smoke effect correct. Outdoors the pig would just hover, looking malevolent, but for indoor shows it travelled from front to back of the area on a cable, and at the end of the show a charge inside exploded dramatically. The show featured other inflatables as well: a giant mother, father and children on a sofa, and later also a car, fridge and television set. These were the band's answer to playing vast open venues, bringing the spectacle alive even for those far away at the back.

During the "Sheep" section of the show on the Animals tour small soft model sheep were fired into the audience using a compressed air cannon. Part of the concert also featured an animated film by Gerald Scarfe that was projected on a big screen behind the band, and showed gory effects such as a city flooded with a sea of blood and a decaying head. Perhaps appropriately, one of the venues played in Paris had previously been an abattoir and in Stafford Pink Floyd appeared in a converted livestock market.

Above: Waters' concept for Animals was to illustrate the human condition – which he felt was generally suffering from moral and social decay – and two of the songs that had been intended for *Wish You Were Here* but dropped were now reworked. "Gotta be Crazy" was rewritten into "Dogs", which takes up most of the first side, and "Raving and Drooling" became "Sheep", forming most of the latter half of the second side. Waters said later that he had had the idea for Animals in the back of his mind for years. Many feel that it is Pink Floyd's best work, while others consider it too dark and violent.

Pink Floyd during the Animals tour of 1977. During 1976, Pink Floyd had played no live concerts. They had recently acquired a property in Islington, and part of it was converted into their own recording studio, where they began working on their next album, *Animals*. It was during this process that Roger Waters began to assert his domination over the others and pursue his own agenda, gradually trying to turn Pink Floyd into more of a vehicle for his personal vision than a creative collaboration as it had been in the past. Richard Wright said about the creation of this album later, "I didn't fight very hard to put my stuff on ... I think I played well, but I didn't contribute to the writing of it but I think that also Roger was kind of not letting me do that. This was the start of the whole ego thing in the band." However, although David Gilmour was distracted by having recently become a father for the first time, he collaborated with Waters on "Dogs", which formed nearly the whole of one side of the album.

Flying pigs...

Nick Mason (above) and Snowy White (right) on the In The Flesh tour of 1977 to promote *Animals*. For the tour additional musicians had joined the band: Dick Parry on sax and Terence "Snowy" White on guitar. White played the guitar solo that was used to link the two halves of "Pigs On The Wing" on the eight-track cartridge release of the album. The idea for the album cover for *Animals*, with its pig floating over Battersea Power Station in London, came from Roger Waters. Hipgnosis – who had designed most of Pink Floyd's album covers since *A Saucerful Of Secrets* in 1968 – suggested that they take suitable photographs of the power station and add the pig in later, but Waters wanted to create the real thing. A giant helium-filled inflatable pig was duly commissioned from Eventstructure Research Group in Amsterdam and made in Germany. The plan was to tether it in place over the power station, while a team of photographers took as many shots as possible, but after the pig was successfully inflated and launched the wind caught it and the cables snapped. It proceeded to float across London towards Heathrow airport causing consternation with the authorities and giving at least one commercial airline pilot the shock of his career. Ironically, the shots of the power station without the pig were eventually chosen for the cover because the clouds looked more interesting, so the pig was added in afterwards anyway.

Animals, an answer to punk

David Gilmour (above) and Roger Waters (opposite) on stage in Oakland, California, during the In The Flesh Animals tour. The second half of the 1970s was marked by the rise of punk rock in UK music circles, as an answer to social unrest but also as a backlash against the whole culture of the rock supergroup. Pink Floyd were one of the obvious targets of the punk bands even though – or perhaps because – their own roots lay in the music underground. However, *Animals* was clearly anti-establishment; Waters was master of the cutting lyric and much of the material was a stream of abuse about leaders abusing their powers, the backstabbing ways of the politics, and how citizens blindly follow their leaders. It was quite well received amongst the more radical representatives of the music press, although some more conservative reviewers felt the band had perhaps gone too far this time.

In The Flesh North American tour

Above and opposite: Fans at a rainy day concert in the USA. Unfortunately when the tour moved on to North America the audiences proved to be rowdy and easily over-stimulated so things quickly got out of hand. Masses of youngsters crammed into giant stadiums yelled and screamed throughout the entire concert, and no longer appeared to be listening to the music at all. A pertinent review of one of the UK concerts in the *Financial Times* had said, "It gets easier and easier to review a Pink Floyd concert without mentioning the music ... it is not just the props that create a barrier between Pink Floyd's music and the reviewer, nor even the elusive, but basically inhuman, nature of the music itself. It is the fascination of the Floyd success ..."

Above: Nick Mason on drums, and with Roger Waters (opposite). A review of the US tour in *Rolling Stone* concluded, "... while their music has become more humanistically cynical and melodious, their concerts grow more and more perfunctory and aloof, amounting to little more than a bombastic insult." And the *Louisville Courier Journal* thought, "Music was not really the point of the show last night, though, and if anyone went to hear the precision musicianship Pink Floyd is known for ... they were probably too distracted by the band's trappings ..." Waters was particularly upset at what the concerts had become and came to hate the whole concept of playing such large venues. He finished the tour stressed and close to a nervous breakdown and, as a response, went off alone to write out his feelings, leaving the others to do as they wished without him.

Financial
irregularities at Soldier Field

Opposite and right: David Gilmour performing live on stage in the US. At a concert at Soldier Field in Chicago the box office had documented the sale of 67,000 tickets. However, Pink Floyd came to doubt the figures and quietly hired a helicopter to photograph the crowd during the concert so they could carry out a headcount. It transpired there were nearer 95,000 people attending and the Federal Grand Jury was soon investigating a shortfall in takings of many hundreds of thousands of dollars.

A further US concert, the third of four consecutive nights at New York's premier venue Madison Square Garden, was marred by some thoughtless fans who brought fireworks to celebrate the following date (July 4, US Independence Day) a little early. Several firecrackers were hurled into the audience below from upper tiers, making many people edgy and causing some minor injuries. David Gilmour seemed able to rise above the tension, but Roger Waters quickly became tense and unhappy, and finally yelled at the audience that anyone with fireworks should "just f*** off and let us get on with it".

Going solo

During the latter part of 1977 and early 1978, David Gilmour began working on his first solo album. He had written most of the songs for the album himself, and joined up with a couple of his musician friends from Cambridge days, Willie Wilson (on drums and percussion) and Rick Willis (on bass and vocals) to produce and record it in France. The album, *David Gilmour*, was released in May 1978 and did quite well, reaching No.17 in the UK and No.29 in the US charts. Gilmour said in a magazine interview at the time: "This album was important to me in terms of self-respect. At first I didn't think my name was big enough to carry it. Being in a group for so long can be a bit claustrophobic, and I needed to step out from behind Pink Floyd's shadow."

Financial disaster looms

Back in 1973, after Pink Floyd had first begun making serious money from *The Dark Side Of The Moon*, the band had taken on financial company Norton Warburg to handle their investment and tax planning. Throughout much of the seventies the band had continued to earn massive amounts from their concerts and record sales, which Norton Warburg had invested on their behalf to reduce their exposure to high UK income tax. Unfortunately, during 1978 it became apparent that the company had selected a series of high-risk investments—not only for Pink Floyd, but also for their other clients—and in September 1978 Pink Floyd ended their agreement with the company.

Above: Pink Floyd on stage during the 1970s. It was not long before it was established that Norton Warburg had lost nearly £15 million of their clients' money, of which several million had belonged to Pink Floyd. After all the hard work of the previous years, the band members were not only practically bankrupt but still owed the taxman thousands of pounds in income tax against their earnings over the previous few years.

Richard Wright (above left) had also released a solo album in 1978, *Wet Dream*, which was recorded at the same time and in the same studios in France as David Gilmour's effort, but which did not do quite as well as the guitarist's album when it was released in September 1978.

Opposite: Drummer Nick Mason's first solo effort, *Fictitious Sports*, was essentially the work of jazz singer Carla Bley, who wrote all the material and co-produced the album. Although it was recorded during 1979 it was not released until 1981 owing to contractual problems.

September 1978:
Recording of The Wall

A new album was obviously required swiftly to earn some much-needed funds, and Roger Waters produced two demos that he had been working on alone in his home studio. *Bricks In The Wall* and *The Pros And Cons Of Hitchhiking* were both in the very early stages of development, but the band chose the first to work further on, which was based around a theme of personal isolation. The scale of the concept required a double album and Waters also planned a tour and a film to go with it. Although the band had chosen to take the idea forward, neither David Gilmour nor Nick Mason were totally convinced that it would work. However, producer Bob Ezrin was soon brought in to coordinate the album, and he reorganized Waters' material into a different order and convinced the band members that the idea as a whole would hang together. The storyline covered events in the life of a rock star—loosely based on Waters himself—including the death of his father at an early age, an overprotective mother, unpleasant experiences at school, the break-up of his marriage, and the downsides of being on tour. Each of the unpleasant experiences becomes a brick in a wall, which eventually separates the star from his audience. Eventually the star manages to pull the wall down, but the end of the album leads back to the beginning ... indicating a never-ending cycle of hope and despair.

Close up of Roger Waters on stage during the 1970s. It was during the recording of *The Wall* that Pink Floyd's method of collaborating began to fall apart. Roger Waters felt a strong sense of ownership for the material, and had come to believe that musically and intellectually he was in a different place to the others. David Gilmour had strong ideas of his own that he was determined to get across— which Waters interpreted as not being interested in the original concept. Nick Mason was close to Waters but had developed other interests outside Pink Floyd, while Richard Wright was suffering personal problems as his marriage hit the rocks, and was frequently distracted. There was often considerable tension between the four band members and Bob Ezrin often had to act as a mediator between Waters and the others. He succeeded in holding the whole thing together, on occasion championing the greater good of the work even against Waters himself—which sometimes caused tension between the two of them as well.

David Gilmour playing a Fender Telecaster custom guitar. His main guitar during this era was a 1979 black Fender Stratocaster with DiMarzio pickups and a 1962 neck fitted with a rosewood fingerboard, although at one time he had a personal collection of several hundred instruments. In September 2008 Fender Guitars released two versions of their David Gilmour Signature Black Strat model. The "Relic" model Fender Stratocaster™ featured careful distressing to reproduce the wear marks on David's own 30-year-old, much-customized guitar, while the "New Old Stock" model included all the same custom parts but was in brand new condition without any distressing.

A growing sense of alienation

During the late 1970s, Roger Waters, in particular, felt a growing sense of alienation from the audience at concerts, which would soon find its outlet in his compositions. At the start of their career, Pink Floyd had been part of the underground music scene and played small to medium venues to committed fans. After the release of *The Dark Side Of The Moon*, however, they had moved into the mainstream music circuit and now had many, many more fans, so they had been forced to move into much bigger venues for concerts.

The band themselves were not that happy about the necessary change in tour venues; they no longer felt a sense of intimacy with their fans – in fact they often began to feel increasingly isolated from them. The band also regretted having to play more US concerts and neglect their UK following – which was one of the big criticisms levelled at them in the press – but there was no arguing with the figures: a US tour not only earned far more money than a UK one ever could, it also had a very noticeable power to stimulate album sales.

A drummer at work; Nick Mason pictured performing during The Wall Tour. During the process of making *The Wall*, the four members of Pink Floyd had been forced to relocate abroad as tax exiles because of financial problems as a result of the Norton Warburg fiasco. Since they could not work in the UK, much of the album was recorded in Super Bear Studios near Nice in the Côte d'Azur, where David Gilmour and Richard Wright had worked on their solo efforts. This change of venue affected Richard Wright more than the others; as he said at a later date, "The rest of the band's children were young enough to stay with them in France but mine were older and had to go to school. I was missing my children terribly." Relations between the four band members soon became so bad that they were rarely in the studio together, even though they were working to a tight schedule to get the album finished in time. Roger Waters had begun to turn most of his frustration at the way things were progressing toward Richard Wright, who all three of the other band members felt was not really pulling his weight. However, Bob Ezrin said later that in many ways Wright was set up to fail; he did not work well under pressure at the best of times and now he was not being left alone to create in his own time as was usually the case but constantly pushed.

October 1979: Richard Wright leaves Pink Floyd

Things came to a head during the band's customary August break – the record company requested an earlier release for the album in time for Christmas, so Waters suggested that Wright should go to Cherokee Studios in Los Angeles before the others to record his keyboard parts, most of which were still not done. However, Wright was now in Greece on a long-awaited holiday with his children and refused to leave them early. Waters was furious at Wright's apparent lack of commitment and – although David Gilmour tried to defuse the situation – he quickly decided that Wright must leave the band and presented an ultimatum: leave quietly but keep a share of the royalties, or be taken to court. At first Wright held firm, but the realities of the band's poor financial situation and the impact a court case could have on his personal finances soon made him realize that he had little choice, although for the moment his departure was kept quiet officially. The first official indication that he had left the band was that his name was completely missing from the credits on *The Final Cut* – he was not involved in its production nor did he perform on it – although full details about his departure were not officially confirmed to the press until 2000.

Guitarist Snowy White, who had appeared with Pink Floyd during the In The Flesh tour of 1977 to promote *Animals*, was again invited to join the line up for the forthcoming tour of *The Wall*, although he had not played on the album. The first song featured session musicians each wearing rubber face masks taken from the real band members; White was "David Gilmour", Andy Bown played "Roger Waters" on bass guitar, Willie Wilson played "Nick Mason" on drums, and Peter Woods was "Richard Wright" on keyboards. After the genuine band took to the stage, the surrogate band removed their masks and then performed back up for the remainder of the show. At around the same time White was invited to become a full time member of Thin Lizzy, so he only performed on the 1980 section of the tour, being replaced on guitars by Andy Roberts when the tour was resurrected in 1981.

Comfortably Numb

David Gilmour on stage in 1980 during The Wall Tour. One of the few tracks on *The Wall* that had a co-credit, "Comfortably Numb", featured music by David Gilmour with lyrics by Roger Waters. Gilmour had written most of the track for his own solo album, but in the end it had not been used so he brought it to *The Wall* recording sessions. He later said, "I think things like 'Comfortably Numb' were the last embers of mine and Roger's ability to work collaboratively together." It caused major arguments between the two, as they disagreed on how the song should be recorded; in the end they selected Waters' version for the beginning and Gilmour's for the end. The song covers a section of the main storyline in which Pink is drugged by his manager to enable him to perform, apparently based on an incident in Waters' career in which he had been given a tranquillizer for stomach cramps before a concert on the Animals tour. The beginning and end of the track feature guitar solos by Gilmour, one of which was voted 4th Best Guitar Solo of All Time by *Guitar World* magazine, and Greatest Guitar Solo of All Time in a poll of listeners of the digital radio station Planet Rock.

Alienation
proves a great success

Richard Wright, Roger Waters, David
Gilmour and Nick Mason fooling
around on The Wall Tour set before
a performance in Los Angeles in
1980. The Floyd's record company
had initially not been that
enthusiastic about *The Wall*, and
first reviews were by no means 100
per cent positive: *Rolling Stone* said,
"*The Wall* is a stunning synthesis of
Waters' by now familiar thematic
obsessions", while *Melody Maker*
said, "I'm not sure whether it's
brilliant or terrible, but I find it
utterly compelling." However, the
album went on to become
outstandingly successful, topping
the Billboard album charts for 15
weeks and becoming one of Pink
Floyd's best-selling albums in the
US second only to *The Dark Side Of
The Moon*.

David Gilmour and Nick Mason playing around for the cameras. When "Another Brick In The Wall Part II" had been recorded for the album it was felt that more variation was needed so the two verses were not exactly the same, and it was decided to include schoolchildren singing as well. Engineer Nick Griffiths in the band's UK studios worked with the head of music at nearby Islington Green School to record small groups of pupils, asking them to shout rather than sing. He then multi-tracked the voices to make it appear as though the groups were much larger. The single became a Christmas No.1 hit around the world, which led some members of the press to claim that children had been taken advantage of by a multi-millionaire rock band since they had not been given a contract for royalties. However, a donation of £1,000 was made to the school and the children later received broadcast royalties under UK law.

Casual portrait of David Gilmour, during the 1980s. For the performance of "Comfortably Numb", Waters sang his opening verse on stage while David Gilmour waited hidden in the darkness at the top of the wall until the cue for his guitar solo, when he was suddenly picked out with a spotlight. Towards the end of the concert the wall across the stage collapses, and additional speakers hidden beneath the auditorium seats gave the distinct impression that the entire venue was collapsing around the audience's ears. Although Richard Wright had officially left Pink Floyd, he continued to play with the band for live performances as a paid session musician. Ironically, he was the only one of them to make any money from The Wall Tour, since the immense cost of the staging meant that overall it made a loss.

The Wall built

For the live performances on tour, the staging was vast and ambitious. A vast real wall was gradually constructed from enormous cardboard bricks as the concert played out, ending with a structure that was some 40 feet (12 metres) high and the width of the stage. At the back, the huge circular screen was also used again for projected images until it was concealed by the growing height of the wall in front.

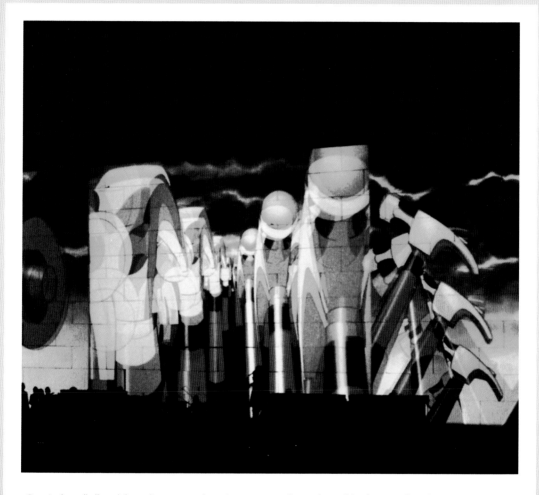

Gaps in the wall allowed the audience to see the various scenes in the story, and as it filled the stage it was also used as a giant screen for the specially commissioned nightmarish animations from Gerald Scarfe to be reproduced, often in triplicate. Three of the characters from the story – the mother, school teacher and wife – were realized as giant inflatables, and there was also another version of the pig that careered wildly across the stage during "Run Like Hell".

May 1982: *The Wall* — the movie

A film of the album was also made, directed by Alan Parker, which was originally going to be a mixture of live concert footage and animations by Gerald Scarfe. Roger Waters was producer on the movie but he and Parker often had conflicting viewpoints; their volatile relationship caused many arguments until Parker persuaded Waters to take a six-week holiday so he could work without interference. Unfortunately it did not prove possible to achieve good enough results by filming the concerts themselves, so the animation segments were retained but the story was told using professional actors, with singer Bob Geldof playing the lead character, Pink.

The world première of *The Wall* movie was at the Cannes Film Festival, where it was generally well received as a powerful depiction of rock music in action. A few critics were critical of some of the military-style scenes, claiming that they appeared to encourage neo-Nazism, while others felt the whole movie battered the senses. Waters later said, "If I'd have directed it – which I'd never have done – it would have been much quieter than it is. He [Parker] paints in fairly bold strokes; he is very worried about boring his audience. It suits us very well, because we did want a lot of this to be a punch in the face."

Despite appearances, like the wall itself the relationship between the various members of Pink Floyd was on the verge of collapse. The Wall Tour was not booked to play any stadiums in the US – venues were restricted to indoor arenas – but the band were offered a million dollars to play two dates at the JFK stadium in Philadelphia. However, it was the experience of playing stadiums like this in 1977 that had brought Roger Waters to the brink of nervous collapse –

which in turn had brought forth the whole concept of *The Wall* – so Waters flatly refused to even consider the offer. The others were keen, and even considered getting someone else to sing Roger's part, but in the end reluctantly agreed that it could not be done. There were only six concerts in the UK, because the band were still not able to spend too much time in the country.

Recording *The Final Cut*

Pink Floyd at Earls Court in August 1980. The band were also contracted to release a soundtrack album of *The Wall* movie, but the problem was that the movie itself had been closely based on the original *Wall* album. One new song had been written: "When The Tigers Broke Free", which was inspired by the death of Waters' father in the Second World War and acted as an overture to the film. To resolve this, they decided to include some music written for the movie but cut out before it was released, plus the new version of "Outside The Wall" that had been created to end the movie. However,

Waters then decided to include other new tracks that he had written about the Falkland Islands conflict. In the past, all band members had a say on new material and if the majority were not convinced of its merit it would be dropped, but now Waters felt that he should be in full control. The others felt that their point of view – and the spirit of compromise within the group that had been so important in the past – was being ignored, and they were not about to accept this lightly, particularly David Gilmour.

March 1983: Release of *The Final Cut*

Interviewed in June 1987, Roger Waters said: "*The Final Cut* was absolutely misery to make, although I listened to it of late and I rather like a lot of it. But I don't like my singing on it. You can hear the mad tension running through it all. If you're trying to express something and being prevented from doing it because you're so uptight ... It was a horrible time. We were all fighting like cats and dogs. We were finally realising — or accepting, if you like — that there was no band. It was really being thrust upon us that we were not a band and had not been in accord for a long time. Not since 1975, when we made *Wish You Were Here*. Even then there were big disagreements about content and how to put the record together."

Tired of the endless rows, David Gilmour (right) had eventually agreed to perform on the new tracks as required, but insisted that his name be taken off the production credits since he felt the material was not what Pink Floyd, as a group, should be doing. Nick Mason had also distanced himself from the growing problems within the band, since he was in the midst of dealing with problems in his marriage. This effectively allowed Roger Waters a free hand to do as he wished, with the other members of the band just performing whatever they were given. Waters may have believed that this meant they had capitulated totally, but he was soon to realize that this was not the case. The album reached the No.1 spot in the UK, but sold poorly in the US and worldwide. Reviews were also mixed: *NME* said, "Underneath the whimpering meditation and exasperated cries of rage it is the old, familiar rock beast: a man who is unhappy in his work." and *Melody Maker* hailed it as "... a milestone in the history of awfulness". But Rolling Stone thought it was "... essentially a Roger Waters solo album ... a superlative achievement on several levels". The album's poor performance confirmed to Gilmour that he was right to dislike much of its material. Some of the tracks that had been included had been dropped from the previous album, *The Wall*, and Gilmour felt they had been left out for good reason: "I said to Roger, 'If these songs weren't good enough for *The Wall*, why are they good enough now?'"

July 13 1985: Live Aid

David Gilmour was the only member of Pink Floyd to appear at Live Aid, playing guitar as part of Bryan Ferry's band and in the "Do They Know It's Christmas?" finale. After the release of his solo album in 1984, Gilmour had embarked on an extensive solo tour to promote it. The tour staging was very simple, with a pared down set and straightforward lighting – very unlike the spectacle offered by a Pink Floyd tour concert. In fact Pink Floyd were unusual in that although the band itself was regarded as one of rock's supergroups, none of the members were really that well known individually except to hard core Floyd fans. This meant that when Waters, Gilmour, Mason and Wright appeared solo, not one of them was automatically recognized as being "Pink Floyd" – so individually they could not generate the level of ticket sales that might have been expected from their fame as a group.

For the first time in their career Pink Floyd decided that they would not tour their new album, *The Final Cut*, and there was also no new album in development, which left the remainder of 1983, 1984 and much of 1985 free. However, each of the three official band members, as well as Richard Wright, produced their own albums during this period – either solo or in collaboration with other musicians. David Gilmour began working on *About Face*, which included performances from other musicians he admired. Gilmour himself wrote many of the tracks featured on the album, but two of them were co-written with his long-time friend Pete Townshend of The Who. The album was released on March 5, 1984, reaching No.21 in the UK charts and No.32 in the US, and was later certified Gold. Meanwhile, Roger Waters completed *The Pros*

And Cons Of Hitch Hiking which was based on his alternative suggestion for Pink Floyd's 1979 album. The album also featured guitarist Eric Clapton and jazz saxophonist David Sanborn and was released on April 16, 1984. It reached No.13 in the UK charts and No.31 in the US. Following its release Waters toured to promote the album. Drummer Nick Mason began what was to become a long-term collaboration with ex-10cc guitarist Rick Fenn, which began with the pair recording a joint album, *Profiles*, at Pink Floyd's Britannia Row studios and Fenn's Basement Studios. Almost all the tracks on the album were instrumentals, but Mason's band-mate David Gilmour sang on "Lie For A Lie", along with singer Maggie Reilly, and another song featured Danny Peyronel from UFO. Mason's album was released on August 19, 1985.

Pink Floyd loses another member

Nick Mason, David Gilmour and Richard Wright. In late 1985, after he returned from his solo US tour, Roger Waters decided that Pink Floyd was a "spent force creatively" and he told EMI and CBS Records that he no longer wished to record with the others – or anyone else – as Pink Floyd. He apparently believed that this would mark the end of Pink Floyd, but he soon found out he was wrong. David Gilmour did not feel it was Waters' decision to terminate the band without any discussion with the two other members – after all Gilmour had been a part of Pink Floyd for nearly 17 years and Mason for 20 years. And Gilmour also didn't accept that there was any reason why a band that still had recording contracts in place should be put out of existence just because one person no longer wanted to be a member. It was pointed out to Waters that if he prevented the others from fulfilling their contracts he would be laying all three band members open to law suits and could be held responsible for everyone's legal expenses. As a result Waters decided to officially resign from Pink Floyd since, as he said, "the financial repercussions would have wiped me out completely". It was almost an eerie repeat of the position that Richard Wright had found himself in, when he was forced out of the band by Waters back in 1979.

The fight to keep Pink Floyd alive

David Gilmour (left) and Richard Wright (far right) on stage in the 1980s. Despite his resignation, Waters apparently still thought that the others would not be able to continue without him. Things came to a head nearly a year later when he discovered that Gilmour and Mason had opened a new bank account and begun planning a new Pink Floyd album. Within days he had made an application to the High Court to prevent the Pink Floyd name being used in the future. His case was based on the fact that Pink Floyd had originally consisted of Syd Barrett, Richard Wright, himself, and Nick Mason; his view was that now the first three founding members had left, it was not reasonable for Mason and Gilmour to continue on as Pink Floyd. He also believed that since he had written most of the lyrics and much of the music for the band since Syd Barrett had left, essentially he was "Pink Floyd". However, as Gilmour commented in an article in the UK newspaper the *Sunday Times*, "no one else has claimed Pink Floyd was entirely them. Anybody who does is extremely arrogant." The legal battles and sniping in the press became quite vicious, leading the fans to wonder if this really was the end of Pink Floyd. Eventually, however, Waters withdrew his legal action: he had written the soundtrack for *When The Wind Blows*, which was due to be released by rival record label Virgin Records – but EMI only agreed to allow this if Waters promised not to interfere with the continuing existence of Pink Floyd.

A new Pink Floyd

After Roger Waters left Pink Floyd, the new set up consisted of David Gilmour (left) and Nick Mason (right), since Richard Wright (centre) could not rejoin the group officially until certain legal complications had been resolved. Although the fans were eager for a new tour, Gilmour and Mason thought that the best option to prove that Pink Floyd was still a going concern would be a brand new album of fresh material, rather than just doing a tour based on their previous hits. It was perhaps also not possible to perform the old material until a final agreement with Roger Waters had been signed, detailing which of them had rights to what and how they were to handle revenue from the historic Floyd material. Gilmour and Mason began working on the new album in late 1986, working on Gilmour's studio houseboat *Astoria*, which was moored on the river Thames at

Hampton, Middlesex. It was based on material that Gilmour had already collected, with the idea of doing another solo album but which he now decided would become a Pink Floyd project. One big obstacle was that Waters had always provided most of the lyrics in the past – and Gilmour later admitted that Waters' absence was a problem and that the new project was difficult without his presence. Several other writers were tried out to help with the lyrics, including modern poet Roger McGough and songwriters Eric Stewart and Carole Pope. However, in the end most of the songs on the album were credited to Gilmour alone, with a few co-written by Anthony Moore, Bob Ezrin – who also co-produced the album – Jon Carin, Phil Manzanera or Patrick Leonard.

A Momentary Lapse Of Reason

On September 7, 1987, a new Floyd album, eagerly anticipated by the fans, was released – nearly four years after the last Pink Floyd album. Although the original intention had been to produce another concept album, Gilmour couldn't make this work successfully so in the end *A Momentary Lapse of Reason* was a collection of unrelated tracks. Gilmour believed that it marked a return to the Floyd of older days – he felt that during the final few years of Roger Waters' time with the band the lyrics had become more important than the music, but that with this new album the lyrics and music had equal emphasis. In an interview at the time he said, *"The Dark Side of the Moon* and *Wish You Were Here* were so successful not just because of Roger's contributions, but also because there was a better balance between the music and the lyrics."* The fans seemed to agree; the album went straight to No.3 in both the UK and the US and had soon sold significantly better than *The Final Cut*. The album was a big success at giving all the members of the band real confidence in their ability to continue on as Pink Floyd without Waters.

September 1987:
A Momentary Lapse Of Reason goes on tour

A tour to promote the album had been planned pretty much from the beginning, although at first it was by no means certain that promoters would be willing to take on the risk. After all, it had been over six years since Pink Floyd had been on tour, and Waters had reportedly tried to stop this new one, contacting various promoters and threatening to sue if they advertised concerts using the Pink Floyd name. The band also knew they had to give the fans the kind of spectacle expected from a Floyd concert, which meant expensive and complex staging, along with breathtaking special effects. To pay for it all, both Gilmour and Mason

invested millions of their own money. In the event Canadian promoter Michael Cohl was the first to buy in to the concept, committing to a single concert in Toronto on September 27, 1987. His confidence was vindicated when all 60,000 tickets were snapped up immediately they went on sale in the fastest sell-out in the history of the venue. A second and then a third show were added at the same venue, both of which sold out nearly as fast. After that, promoters across America were clamouring to take dates on the tour, which was soon booked to run through to the end of 1987.

The A Momentary Lapse of Reason Tour kicked off two days after the release of the album with a concert in Ontario, Canada on September 9, 1987. Due to the ongoing legal complications Richard Wright was continuing to play as a salaried musician, but from the fans' point of view Pink Floyd was alive and rocking, still with three of its members. A massive success, the tour continually broke box office records for ticket sales across the US and easily out-performed the pulling power of any other group's US tour that year. It then went on to New Zealand, Australia, Japan, across North America again, round Europe and finally back to North America, for a total of 200 concerts, finishing in July 1989. Although critics were divided on the merits of some of the new pieces – and some commented on the lack of animation sometimes shown by Mason and Wright on stage – it was generally agreed that experiencing the vintage Floyd material in a concert was an aural and visual treat that no true fan should miss. As it turned out, Waters was touring the US at pretty much the same time as his former band mates, taking his Radio Kaos tour to smaller venues often within days of a nearby Pink Floyd stadium concert. Some newspapers took pleasure in commenting on the fact that Waters was playing to smaller audiences, perhaps forgetting that he had earlier refused to consider playing massive stadium dates ever again. Waters also played some of the old Floyd classics alongside his newer material, so the winners in the ongoing feud between the two factions were certainly the fans, who enjoyed twice as much Floyd material after the dearth of the last few years.

December 1987:
A business arrangement

Even after the court case regarding the Pink
Floyd name had been dropped, recording
sessions for *A Momentary Lapse of Reason*
on the *Astoria* had often been interrupted
by phone calls from lawyers, as Waters and
the other band members attempted to sort
out their differences. Although Waters was
no longer a member of the band, he was
still a shareholder and director of Pink
Floyd music and so had some say in the
band's financial affairs. Waters had
attempted to block whatever the others
wished to do at every opportunity, but
eventually decided that he had had enough
of all the arguments. On December 23, he
and the others met on David Gilmour's
houseboat, *Astoria*, and finally came to an
agreement as to how Pink Floyd's business
affairs would be handled. Mason and
Gilmour were allowed to continue to use
the Pink Floyd name, while Waters was
granted rights to *The Wall* and to the use of
the "flying pig" image, amongst other
things. Despite the agreement, relations
between the two factions were to remain
poor for many years to come.

Rock in space

David Gilmour with Patty Smyth at a party thrown for guitarist Les Paul at the Hard Rock Cafe in New York in August 1988. In November of that year Pink Floyd released a double live album, *Delicate Sound of Thunder*, taken from recordings of their 1988 concerts in Long Island during the Lapse of Reason Tour. A cassette of this album was taken into space by the three-man crew of a rocket bound for the Russian space station Mir, thus officially becoming the first rock music to be heard in space.

Les Paul and David Gilmour on stage during a Les Paul tribute concert, Les Paul & Friends, at the Brooklyn Academy of Music in Brooklyn, New York, during August 1988. Les Paul, a player, inventor and recording artist, built his first solid-body electric guitar in 1941, and continued to make refinements to his prototype throughout the decade. The guitar that bears his name – the Gibson Les Paul – grew out of his desire as a musician to create a stringed instrument that could make electronic sound without distortion. Paul had been inducted into the US Rock And Roll Hall Of Fame in 1988 and had recently returned to performing live although now in his seventies.

David Gilmour with British singer Kate Bush in 1990. Gilmour had first been introduced to a teenage Bush in the early 1970s, after receiving an amateur demo tape of her songs from a mutual friend. He helped her produce a professionally recorded demo tape, which he brought to the attention of EMI and which led to the record label offering her a recording contract even though she was still at school. Bush went on to become one of the UK's most successful solo female performers, and Gilmour later often played on her songs.

A solo career

Roger Waters pictured in 1990, around the time that he staged The Wall – Live In Berlin in Berlin's Potsdamerplatz with a variety of guest artistes on behalf of the Memorial Fund For Disaster Relief. Many years after he left Pink Floyd in 1985 Roger Waters defended his actions during recording of *The Final Cut*, pointing out that he had never told the others that they could not contribute – but that he was a prolific writer while the others did not produce very much material at all. He therefore felt that it was left to him to fill the albums. It was certainly true that Nick Mason had never been interested in writing new material, and while both David Gilmour and Richard Wright produced excellent material there had never been much of it. In hindsight, even David Gilmour conceded that Waters had a point: he said later, "I'm certainly guilty at times of being lazy, and moments have arrived when Roger might say, 'Well, what have you got?' And I'd be like, 'Well, I haven't got anything right now. I need a bit of time to put some ideas on tape.'"

Richard Wright performing with Pink Floyd in 2006 – he had officially returned to the band after the end of the Lapse of Reason Tour. Back in April 1984 he had released a second solo album, *Identity*, in collaboration with musician Dave Harris – Wright had contributed the music and Harris the lyrics. Almost all the tracks were composed and performed on the Fairlight computer; looking back on it later Wright came to feel that it was an interesting experiment although many Floyd fans were disappointed that it had not been more like his first solo album. In 1991 he and Gilmour recorded some instrumentals for a classic-car racing film, *La Carrera Panamericana*, set in Mexico and featuring Gilmour and Mason as participating drivers. The movie was released in 1992.

David Gilmour performing in the late 1990s. In 1990 Gilmour established the Intrepid Aviation Company to manage his collection of vintage aircraft, which were often leased to movie production companies for filming. Some years later he decided to sell Intrepid, because – as he told a BBC radio interviewer – "Intrepid Aviation was a way for me to make my hobby pay for itself a little bit, but gradually over a few years Intrepid Aviation became a business because you have to be businesslike about it. Suddenly I found instead of it being a hobby and me enjoying myself, it was a business and so I sold it. I don't have Intrepid Aviation any more. I just have a nice old biplane that I pop up, wander around the skies in sometimes ..."

Part Three

The Division Bell

1993: Recording *The Division Bell*

Work began on tracks for a new Floyd album in early 1993. Its title, *The Division Bell*, was inspired by the bell in the UK House of Commons, which calls members into the chamber to vote – some saw it as signifying that it was time for fans to decide, or vote, on whether they were for or against the new Floyd. By this time both Richard Wright and Nick Mason were fully back on form and the band had hit its stride so the album was a resounding success, becoming one of the band's most successful albums to date. Its theme was the problem of communication – both personal communication between friends or lovers, and global communication between rival factions. Richard Wright co-wrote "Wearing The Inside Out", achieving his first writing credit since 1975, but much of the other material was co-written by Polly Samson, a journalist who was now Gilmour's new wife. The Division Bell Tour featured a mixture of Floyd material from across the years, with different play lists at different venues – the entire *The Dark Side Of The Moon* was played at some concerts, while others featured individual songs not necessarily in any set order. The concerts featured the usual large stage, circular screen, incredible special effects, quadrophonic sound and powerful lasers – and to keep the tour moving, three stages leapfrogged around North America and Europe, each 180 feet long and featuring a 130 foot arch modelled on the Hollywood Bowl. The Division Bell Tour became the first tour ever to gross over US$100 million in the US after only 59 concerts. Worldwide, it played to an estimated 5.5 million people in 68 cities and grossed over US$ 250 million.

David Gilmour (opposite) and Roger Waters (right): *The Division Bell* turned out to be Pink Floyd's final studio album, although in 1995 they released a live album, *P*U*L*S*E*, which featured songs recorded during concerts in the UK and Europe during The Division Bell Tour, including a complete performance of *The Dark Side of the Moon* as well as selections from *The Wall* and *Wish You Were Here*. The new album quickly hit No.1 in the UK, US and most of the other countries where it was released, and was certified Double Platinum within two months.

The following year, on January 17, 1996, Pink Floyd were inducted into the US Rock And Roll Hall Of Fame in a ceremony at the Waldorf-Astoria Hotel in New York. All three current members of Pink Floyd attended the induction ceremony, but Mason left the stage when Gilmour and Wright sang "Wish You Were Here" along with their presenter Billy Corgan.

Roger Waters on stage during the Glastonbury Festival of Performing Arts in the UK on June 29, 2002. This appearance formed the final date on his In The Flesh European Tour 2002, in front of an estimated 70,000 fans. He performed some Pink Floyd classics, such as "Another Brick In The Wall Part II", "Wish You Were Here' and "Money", as well as a selection of his own more recent material, such as "Amused To Death" and "The Bravery Of Being Out Of Range". Highlights of the festival were filmed for screening on BBC Television. Waters had recently renewed his friendship with Nick Mason, but relationships remained strained with David Gilmour and Richard Wright.

In 2003 David Gilmour sold his London home to Earl Spencer for £3.6m and handed all the proceeds straight to Crisis – the charity for the homeless – to help fund an urban village modelled on a scheme in New York, which aimed to provide rooms for up to 400 homeless people and low-paid key workers in the heart of London. At a press conference Gilmour played down his donation, pointing out that he still had four other properties, including a farmhouse in Sussex and a villa in Greece, and that he and his wife, journalist and author Polly Samson, planned to buy a smaller London mews house instead. He said, "There's nothing quite like having a large house that you don't need to focus your mind on those who have no house at all. Giving the money from the sale of the house to help the homeless was a natural progression of those thoughts." Gilmour went on to become a vice-president of Crisis, helping to collect donations from other celebrity philanthropists.

Nick Mason and his wife Nette at the launch of Mario Testino's latest collection on October 20, 2003, in aid of the Sargent Cancer Care Charity. Pink Floyd were currently in the news in other areas too – on October 13, an extraordinary exhibition about the band, Pink Floyd Interstellar, had opened in Paris. It was mounted with the support and collaboration of Nick Mason, David Gilmour, Richard Wright – and Roger Waters, as well – who had all provided the content from their personal archives. The exhibition was arranged chronologically, mostly with one room per album, with unique exhibits included pages from Syd Barrett's notebook, some of the band's old instruments, inflatables from various tours, and films that had been projected at concerts or that showed the various band members performing. It ran until January 25, 2004.

David Gilmour with daughter Alice (left), second wife Polly (right) and son Charlie (far right) at Buckingham Palace in London on November 7, 2003, after being made a CBE (Commander of the British Empire) by Queen Elizabeth II for his services to music. Gilmour joked that the Queen had probably never even listened to Pink Floyd.

"I suspect that if she has listened to Pink Floyd it has been one of her children or grandchildren playing it and she is more likely to be the one to say 'turn it off'," he said. "But I do not know her taste in music. She said Pink Floyd had been doing it for a very long time and I had to agree. Playing to a hundred thousand people is not so nerve-wracking, playing to a few people is much harder. It was not so bad today, but I was a bit nervous. I hope that primarily it [the CBE] is for what I have done in music, but if some of my recent more publicized charity work has made a difference then I am happy about that."

Appearing for charity

David Gilmour and Mica Paris on stage at the Albert Hall on April 1, 2004, during a concert in the annual series of Teenage Cancer Trust fundraising shows arranged by patron Roger Daltrey of The Who. Other well-known musicians appearing at the concert included Jools Holland, Ronnie Wood and Jeff Beck. Apart from being Vice-President of Crisis, Gilmour is currently regularly involved in several charities, and has performed at many benefit gigs on behalf of the Teenage Cancer Trust, Nordoff-Robbins Music Therapy, Amnesty International, and PETA (People for the Ethical Treatment for Animals), among others.

INSIDE OUT
A PERSONAL HISTORY OF **PINK FLOYD**

Nick Mason at the launch of his memoirs, *Inside Out – A Personal History Of Pink Floyd*, at the Virgin Megastore in West Hollywood in October 2004. He said, "I started making notes for this book in 1994. We had just finished a world tour, and for the first time in many months I was not involved in trying to stuff another bundle of free T-shirts, tour jackets, hotel soaps and towelling robes into my suitcase. With a certain amount of leisure time beckoning, I thought it might be time to start dealing with the questions I'd been asked for thirty-odd years – 'How did the band get its name?', 'Where's Syd?' and 'What's it really like?'. It's only taken ten years to come up with some answers. I eventually decided to avoid a rundown of every gig, venue, weather condition and moustache. To be frank that seemed exquisitely dull, and threatened to become drudgery. What I hope has emerged is a personal take on the band's history, with help from some intense fans, virtuous friends and helpful colleagues. Everyone, inevitably, has a different – often very different – view of what really took place. I've simply tried to capture the elements that I think give a picture of what I thought was happening at any one time, and to try to be honest about both the triumphs and the complete shambles that make up a band's existence. Above all, *Inside Out* is about being part of a band – shared experiences that stretch across four decades, the whole of my adult life."

2005: Live 8

David Gilmour, Roger Waters, Nick Mason and Richard Wright are reunited for a performance at Live 8 London in London's Hyde Park on July 2, 2005, the first time the four had been on stage together for 24 years. Although the reunion had been orchestrated by Bob Geldof, Nick Mason later said, "You can't carry on World War Three forever. If we hadn't reformed for Live 8, we'd have done it for another charity event, I suspect." The news that the four of them would all appear together was officially confirmed on June 12, and it caused tremendous excitement amongst Pink Floyd's loyal fans. Applications for free tickets had to be submitted by mobile phone lottery, but this closed within 24 hours so there was little prospect for overseas fans to see the band perform. A black market in the onward sale of the free tickets quickly sprang up, despite the organizers' attempts to stop it.

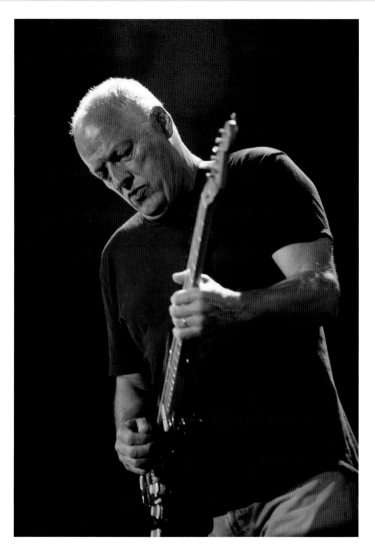

The nine other simultaneous Live 8 shows were held in Philadelphia, Berlin, Rome, Paris, Barrie, Tokyo, Cornwall, Moscow and Johannesburg, with a final concert on July 6 in Murrayfield Stadium, Edinburgh, Scotland. Live 8 involved 150 bands and 1,250 musicians playing across the globe and the date had been selected to precede the G8 Summit that was being held at the Gleneagles Hotel in Scotland a few days later. The aim was to ask people not to give money but their names for inclusion on the Live 8 List, which aimed to persuade G8 leaders to make a firm commitment to relieve poverty and increase aid to the Third World. Bob Geldof had decided to ask Pink Floyd if they would play together at the event, since their records were still immensely popular – particularly in North America – even though some members of the band had not spoken to each other for years. He called Roger Waters, who was immediately enthusiastic and soon made his own call to David Gilmour.

Opposite: Roger Waters in full flow at Live 8 London. Pink Floyd took to the stage around 11.00pm and performed four songs: "Speak To Me/Breathe/Breathe (Reprise)", "Money", "Wish You Were Here" and "Comfortably Numb", with Gilmour and Waters sharing lead vocals. Before the start of "Wish You Were Here," Waters spoke to the audience: "It's actually quite emotional, standing up here with these three guys after all these years, standing to be counted with the rest of you. Anyway, we're doing this for everyone who's not here, and particularly of course for Syd."

Above: Richard Wright performing at Live 8 London. Wright was one of the few Pink Floyd members who did not make official statements about the reunion, although he was very happy to perform at the event. Asked about it later, he said he would be happy on stage anywhere and that his plan was to "meander" along and to play whenever he was asked.

Nick Mason, David Gilmour, Richard Wright and Roger Waters at Live 8. Roger Waters later said, "It was more fun than I can remember having with Pink Floyd twenty-five years ago. I was there to enjoy myself." Before they came on stage Pink Floyd had been introduced by their by now iconic "cardiograph blip", which moved at speed across the screens at the sides and back of the stage. In the opinion of many critics, they went on to turn in one of their best-ever performances at the event, which apart from the live UK audience was also broadcast to millions of other Floyd fans across the world. A whole generation of younger music lovers was also introduced to Floyd music for the first time, and went on to become confirmed fans.

David Gilmour playing at Live 8. His official statement about the event as reported by the BBC had said, "Like most people I want to do everything I can to persuade the G8 leaders to make huge commitments to the relief of poverty ... Any squabbles Roger and the band have had in the past are so petty in this context, and if reforming for this concert will help focus attention then it's got to be worthwhile." After the event he reportedly sent Roger Waters an email that said, "Hi Rog, I'm glad you made that phone call. It was fun, wasn't it?" David Gilmour, Nick Mason and Roger Waters during their Live 8 London performance. In a summing up of the event, BBC journalist Ian Youngs said of the Floyd's performance, "If there was one historic musical moment, this was it – the reconciliation of Dave Gilmour and Roger Waters. They looked like they had never been away and the sublime magnificence of their songs swept across the audience."

An estimated crowd of 250,000 music lovers filled the Hyde Park concert area. Those not lucky enough to get tickets to Hyde Park were able to watch the show and share in the excitement on giant BBC screens that were installed in the centre of major cities across the UK, including Birmingham, Hull, Liverpool, Manchester, Plymouth, Portsmouth, Belfast, Leeds, and Wrexham. The UN Secretary General Kofi Annan told the crowd in London: "This is really a United Nations. The whole world has come together in solidarity with the poor. On behalf of the poor, the voiceless and the weak I say thank you."

Guitarist Tim Renwick with Pink Floyd on stage – other musicians who appeared as the Floyd's backing band at the event included Jon Carin on keyboards, and Dick Parry on sax, while Carol Kenyon provided backing vocals. Roger Waters had rehearsed with the other band members for only three days before their Live 8 London appearance, but they chose to cut out much of the fancywork that had been added over time and take things back to how they had performed together in the early days. Roger Waters said later that he had decided beforehand that if there were any differences of opinion in rehearsals he would be the one to take a step back, so potential arguments were kept to a minimum.

The image of Pink Floyd's group hug at the close of their set became one of the most famous images from Live 8 – David Gilmour had originally begun to leave the stage after thanking the audience, but Waters called him back. After the concert, relations between the band members had mellowed considerably – although both Gilmour and Waters ruled out any idea of playing another tour together. Gilmour later said that Pink Floyd was over, and that Live 8 was just a good way to achieve closure, while Waters was adamant that he wasn't remotely tempted because he didn't need the money and wasn't interested in the prospect of having to back down on his own ideas for more than a one-off concert.

During the course of the campaign over 30 million people from all around the world gave their names for the Live 8 list, which was presented to the British Prime Minister Tony Blair, the 2005 chair of the G8 conference. In the week following the performance there was a considerable revival of interest in Pink Floyd, with a significant increase in sales of *Echoes: The*

Best Of Pink Floyd and *The Wall*, but Gilmour decided to donate his share of any increased profits to charity. His lead was quickly followed by many other major stars who had appeared at the event, including The Who, Paul McCartney and Annie Lennox.

November 2005: UK Music Hall Of Fame

Nick Mason and David Gilmour receive the induction award on behalf of Pink Floyd on stage during the final of the UK Music Hall of Fame in 2005, which was broadcast live from Alexandra Palace in London on UK's Channel 4 Television. The award show was the culmination of a two-week television series that had looked at popular music of the 1950s–90s and the acts included in the show had been selected by a panel of more than 60 artists, journalists, broadcasters and executives. Pink Floyd accepted their induction award from Pete Townshend of The Who. Richard Wright was unable to attend, since he had recently had an eye operation, and Roger Waters was attending the opening of his opera, *Ça Ira*, in Rome although he appeared in a video link.

July 2006: Syd Barrett leaves the stage

Richard Wright, David Gilmour and Nick Mason at the DVD première of the movie *Pulse* in London's West End in July. In the same month, on July 7, 2006, their old friend and band mate Syd Barrett died at the age of 60 from pancreatic cancer, although his death has usually been reported as due to "complications from diabetes". After his death his home in St Margaret's Square was placed on the market and reportedly attracted considerable interest but after over 100 viewings – many by fans – it was sold to a French couple who apparently knew nothing about Barrett and bought the house simply because they liked it. Barrett left approximately £1.25 million to his two brothers and two sisters, which had largely been acquired via royalties from Pink Floyd compilations and live recordings that had featured songs he had written whilst with the band. In May 2007 a tribute concert was held at the Barbican Centre, London, at which the four remaining members of Pink Floyd performed – although not all on stage at the same time.

David Gilmour and Richard Wright in Germany in July 2006. This was to be one of Wright's last official Pink Floyd appearances, as on September 15, 2008, he died of cancer at his home in the UK. David Gilmour said in a tribute to his lost band mate, "No one can replace Richard Wright. He was my musical partner and my friend. In the welter of arguments about who or what was Pink Floyd, Rick's enormous input was frequently forgotten. He was gentle, unassuming and private but his soulful voice and playing were vital, magical components of our most recognized Pink Floyd sound." And Roger Waters agreed, "... it is hard to overstate the importance of his musical voice in the Pink Floyd of the '60s and '70s ... Rick's ear for harmonic progression was our bedrock."

Out And About in 2006

Nick Mason with his two sons and his wife Nette, at the UK première of *Sixty-six* in Leicester Square, London, on October 23, 2006. Earlier that year he had played drums on *The Dark Side Of The Moon* during selected dates of Roger Waters' European Summer Festival Tour and the following US Autumn Tour. A serious auto-buff, Mason had been invited by Ferrari to purchase one of their 400 Enzos, which *Top Gear* presenter Jeremy Clarkson persuaded him to lend so the BBC programme could review it. Mason agreed, on the sole condition that Clarkson promoted the recent release of his book *Inside Out*. As a result, Clarkson used Pink Floyd album titles in his description of the Enzo and *Top Gear* test driver The Stig was shown driving round the track with "Another Brick In The Wall" playing – even though the Enzo was not equipped with a stereo. Mason later sold his Enzo to millionaire Mohammad Jamil for £650,000.

David Gilmour and his wife Polly Samson arrive at Alexandra Palace in London on November 14 for the UK Music Hall of Fame 2006. Earlier that year Gilmour had released *On An Island*, his third solo album after a gap of 22 years. Much of the album was recorded in Gilmour's private studio aboard his houseboat *Astoria*, and it featured fellow Floyd member Richard Wright – in his last recorded performance before he died – as well as Robert Wyatt, Jools Holland and Georgie Fame. The album entered the UK charts at No.1 and reached the top spot in Europe too, as well as being the first Gilmour solo album to reach the Top 10 in the US. It went on to sell over a million copies and in 2009 was chosen as The Greatest Solo Album by a Former Band Member by classic rock station Planet Rock.

David Gilmour with Brian Wilson of The Beach Boys at the third UK Music Hall of Fame ceremony at Alexandra Palace, London, in November 2006, after Gilmour had inducted Wilson. It turned out to be the last such induction ceremony that was held, since there were no inductees in 2007 and it was announced in September 2008 that sponsors Channel 4 had axed the ceremony. The following month, two new versions of the early Pink Floyd hit "Arnold Layne" were released, one featuring David Bowie on lead vocals and the other with Richard Wright; both had been recorded in May 2005.

A new world tour

Roger Waters on stage in Perth during his Dark Side Of The Moon Tour in February 2007. The tour had originally begun in June 2006 with a concert in Lisbon, Portugal – the first dates were played across Europe covering Italy, Germany, The Netherlands, Norway, Greece, Turkey, Israel, Russia, Ireland, England, Denmark, Ukraine, Malta, France and Switzerland. Of the twenty-one concerts on this section of the tour, all but eight were solo shows. Waters' band for the tour included Andy Fairweather-Low and Snowy White on guitar, with Nick Mason as a guest drummer for some dates. The first half of the show was based around a selection of Pink Floyd classics and Waters' solo material. The second half included a complete performance of the Pink Floyd classic *The Dark Side of the Moon*, ending with an encore taken from *The Wall*.

March 2007: Hello, I love you

Roger Waters on stage in Shanghai, in February 2007. After the European leg, the Dark Side Of The Moon Tour had played seventeen venues across the US and in 2007 it moved on to Australia and New Zealand. The Chinese leg of the tour came next, then it went to Europe again, across South America and finally back to the US – the tour did not finish until 2008. In March, Waters released a new single, "Hello, I Love You", which had been written in collaboration with Howard Shore for the 2007 movie *The Last Mimzy*. Waters said of the song, "I think together we've come up with a song that captures the themes of the movie – the clash between humanity's best and worst instincts, and how a child's innocence can win the day."

David Gilmour, Nick Mason and Roger Waters on stage, with Dick Parry on saxophone, during Live 8 in 2005. In 2007, Nick Mason was reported as saying that he wanted Pink Floyd to tour again, partly to keep the band at the forefront of the music industry but also because he wanted to go on the road again. "There are no plans for more Floyd concerts, but I would like to do another one. But it's up to David and Roger. They know how I feel. You need there to be four members. The group certainly hasn't retired for good as far as I'm concerned."

Roger Waters on stage in Hong Kong during the Chinese leg of his Dark Side Of The Moon Tour in February 2007. Waters has not released an album since his opera *Ça Ira* in 2005, which was a piece of classical work – the album before that was *In The Flesh – Live*, which was released in 2000. However, in recent interviews he has said that he has numerous songs already written that he intends to release when he has put together a complete album of material.

Although Roger Waters is known as a bass guitarist and vocalist, he also plays electric guitar – as he did on *Wish You Were Here* and *Animals*. He also frequently plays acoustic guitar during parts of the show on his live tours, mostly on tracks from *The Final Cut* and on "Mother". On the Dark Side Of The Moon Tour his acoustic guitar was a Martin 000-28ECHF Bellezza Nera, as shown here.

Left: David Gilmour, his wife Polly Samson, and Robert Plant arriving at the Odeon, Leicester Square, on September 6, 2007, for the world première of *Remember That Night? David Gilmour Live At The Royal Albert Hall*. A second US première was held just over a week later on September 15. Released across the UK on September 17 as a DVD, *Remember That Night* is a film of Gilmour's live solo concerts at the Albert Hall in London at the end of May 2006.

Opposite: David Gilmour posing for photographers in front of the billboard advertising his new DVD, at the world première screening of *Remember That Night? David Gilmour Live At The Royal Albert Hall* in Leicester Square. A second disc that came with the main DVD had a selection of fascinating bonus material, including extra footage taken at a concert at the Mermaid Theatre in London in March 2006, and part of a documentary filmed backstage between shows in Los Angeles.

Snowy White with Roger Waters in Hong Kong during the Chinese leg of the Dark Side Of The Moon Tour in February 2007. In May 2008, Roger Waters played The Dark Side Of The Moon for the first time it its entirety since performing it with Pink Floyd in the mid-1970s.

In April 2008 Waters' opera, *Ça Ira*, was performed with the libretto in English as part of the Festival Amazonas de Ópera in Brazil. Based on a French libretto by Étienne Roda-Gil and his wife Nadine, the opera told the story of the French Revolution. The recording of the opera, released on September 26, 2005, gave Waters his first solo No.1 hit and the opera was first performed in full in November 2005 in Rome. The work received very good reviews, but has been criticised for the amount of staging it requires – a full performance in Poland used over 500 performers and featured horses, carriages and war scenes with soldiers and stunt performers.

Nick Mason and his wife attending a prize ceremony at Stockholm Concert Hall on August 26, 2008. Both husband and wife race classic cars, and earlier that year they had appeared at VSCC Silverstone – although unfortunately both had to return to the paddock with a certain amount of battle damage. However, as Mason said in his column for *Classic and Performance Car* later, "The good thing was that at least we didn't run into each other, which might really have spoilt the day."

David Gilmour with his wife Polly Samson (left) and Sting (right) at the private view of Alan Aldridge's exhibition The Man With The Kaleidescope Eyes at the Design Centre in London on October 13, 2008. On November 11, 2009, Anglia Ruskin University of Cambridge and Chelmsford awarded Gilmour an Honorary Doctorate: "The Faculty of Arts, Law and Social Sciences is honouring some outstanding figures from the world of music and publishing with Honorary Doctor of Arts awards. David Gilmour attended Cambridgeshire College of Arts and Technology, a part of what is now Anglia Ruskin University ... He is honoured for his outstanding contribution to music as a writer, performer and innovator."

Rock on, Pink Floyd

Opposite: David Gilmour performing at a fundraising evening, Hoping's Got Talent, in aid of the Hoping For Palestine charity, on June 18, 2009, at the Café de Paris in London. Supermodel Kate Moss (front right) performed "Summertime" while Gilmour played guitar, after a guest at the event bid £47,000 to hear the model duet with the rock legend. In total the event raised over £500,000 for the Hoping Foundation – Hoping stands for Hope and Optimism for Palestinians In the Next Generation and aims to raise money for community projects involving children in Palestinian refugee camps.

Above: David Gilmour and Nick Mason, accompanied by their respective wives, attend the Summer Exhibition Preview Party 2009 at the Royal Academy of Arts in London on June 3, 2009. Although the fans still hope for a Pink Floyd reunion with both Gilmour and Waters, this seems increasingly unlikely ...

Chronology

1943

Jul 28   Richard (Rick) William Wright is born in Hatch End in Middlesex, England.

Sep 6   George Roger Waters is born in Great Bookham in Surrey, England.

1944

Jan 27   Nicholas (Nick) Berkeley Mason is born in Birmingham, England.

1946

Jan 6   Roger Keith "Syd" Barrett is born in Cambridge, England.

Mar 6   David (Dave) Jon Gilmour is born in Cambridge, England.

1962-64

Various members of what will become Pink Floyd appear with several different bands in Cambridge and then in London.

1964

Autumn   Roger 'Syd' Barrett, Nick Mason and Roger Waters, along with Rado 'Bob' Klose and Mike Leonard, form a band in London named Leonard's Lodgers, which is later renamed The Spectrum Five and then The Tea Set. They appear at several concerts in colleges and small venues around London and at private parties.

1965

Mar   The band perform a live audition at Beat City in Oxford Street, London, using the name Pink Floyd officially for the first time. The line-up now consists of Syd Barrett, Bob Klose, Nick Mason, Roger Waters and Richard Wright.

During the remainder of 1965 the band appear several times, sometimes billed as Pink Floyd and sometimes as The Tea Set.

1966

Mar 13   As the Pink Floyd Sound, the band gets its first billing at The Marquee, a London club, at one of a series of performance events that come to be dubbed 'Spontaneous Underground'. Pink Floyd is invited back to appear regularly at further events.

Jun 12   Peter Jenner, one of the co-founders of a fledgling music management company, sees Pink Floyd perform at The Marquee.

Late Sep   Peter Jenner and Andrew King sign Pink Floyd to a management contract.

Oct 15   Pink Floyd performs at the International Times All Night Rave at The Roundhouse in London.

Oct 31   At Thompson Recording Studios in Hemel Hempstead, the band record a demo tape.

Nov 18   A 'psychodilia' music event is staged at Hornsey College Of Art featuring Pink Floyd and light show designed by students at the college. Coloured lights go on to become an essential part of Pink Floyd's appearances.

Dec 12   Pink Floyd appears at You're Joking – A Benefit Carnival For Oxfam, at the Royal Albert Hall.

1967

Jan 11–12   Two days of recording at Sound Techniques Studio in Chelsea for the documentary, *Tonite Let's All Make Love in London*. Two of the tracks recorded are "Interstellar Overdrive" and "Nick's Boogie".

Jan 23–25   Three days of recording at Sound Techniques Studio in Chelsea for the band's forthcoming debut single, "Arnold Layne", and the B-side "Candy And A Currant Bun". A further three days of recording take place on January 29 and 31, and February 1.

Jan 27   Granada TV film part of an arts documentary at London's UFO Club, a section of which shows Pink Floyd performing.

Feb 1 Pink Floyd sign a recording contract with EMI Records and so officially turn professional.

Feb 7 Granada ITV's arts documentary *Scene Special* covers the underground music scene, and features Pink Floyd playing at the UFO concert at The Blarney Club in London on January 17.

Feb 21 Start of recording sessions with EMI at their Abbey Road studios to produce Pink Floyd's first album, *The Piper At The Gates Of Dawn*.

Feb/Mar After a feature in UK newspaper *The News Of The World* claims that Pink Floyd's music glorifies drug abuse, causing at least one scheduled live performance to be cancelled, the band goes on record to state that to them the term 'psychedelic' means the use of sound and light as part of their performance and is not meant to promote the use of LSD.

Mar 3 A Press Reception and photo opportunity is held at EMI Records in London on behalf of Pink Floyd.

Mar 10 Reporting the release of Pink Floyd's first single, "Arnold Layne", *Record Retail and Music Industry News* said, "This is rather way out and this group with its tremendous visual impact have already built a big following."

Mar 30 BBC television film Pink Floyd

for the UK's most popular music show, *Top Of The Pops*, but the scheduled broadcast the following week is cancelled reportedly because "Arnold Layne" has failed to reach a high enough position in the charts.

Apr 24 Roger Waters is hurt when a coin is thrown at the band from the audience, causing a deep cut in his forehead.

Apr 29 Pink Floyd play their first overseas gig, a performance that is filmed for broadcast on The Netherlands music show, *Fan Club*, on May 5. The 14 Hour Technicolour Dream is staged London's Alexandra Palace, featuring 30 groups playing for free. 10,000 watch Pink Floyd play at sunrise, after a breakneck journey back from The Netherlands.

May 12 A 'musical and visual exploration' is staged at the Queen Elizabeth Hall in London. Called *Games For May*, Pink Floyd compose a new song for the event, which becomes the basis for their next single "See Emily Play". Their performance features the most complex light show seen in London to date and the first use of quadrophonic sound in the U.K.

May After several days abortive work at EMI Studios in Abbey Road, the band moves to Sound Technique Studios in Chelsea to record "See Emily Play" and "Scarecrow" apparently because

they had been unable to re-create the sound achieved on "Arnold Layne" in a different studio.

Jul 13 Pink Floyd finally make their first appearance on BBC television's *Top Of The Pops* to promote "See Emily Play". The boys wear all their best finery and Syd is immaculate in velvet and satin.

Jul 20 For a second appearance on *Top Of The Pops*, Syd turns up still wearing the same, but now rather crumpled, clothes.

Jul 27 A third and final appearance on *Top Of The Pops*. This time Syd is very unkempt and resists all attempts to make him look more acceptable. It is a first sign of the problems to come as he begins to sink into erratic and often strange behaviour, partly caused by his use of mind-altering drugs.

Aug Several planned concerts are cancelled at the last minute due to Syd's increasingly unpredictable behaviour. The official announcement to the Press is that he is exhausted and has been ordered to rest, and that the rest of the band will use the time for a short vacation.

Aug 7 First of several sessions at EMI Studios in Abbey Road to record tracks for the next album, *A Saucerful of Secrets*.

Sep 9   First concert on a short overseas tour, which starts in Denmark and Sweden, then moves on to Ireland.

Oct 23   The first few scheduled concerts of Pink Floyd's first US tour have to be cancelled after work permits do not arrive in time.

Nov 4   Pink Floyd finally appears for the first time in the US, at the Winterland Auditorium in San Francisco.

Nov 6   The band are recorded playing and are then interviewed for the *Pat Boone In Hollywood* show, but Syd refuses to reply to any questions. The segment is broadcast on KHJ TV on Dec 4.

Nov 7   During an appearance on Dick Clark's *American Bandstand*, Waters has to lip-synch to "See Emily Play" since Syd – lead singer as well as guitarist – is apparently in a world of his own and doesn't open his mouth. The segment is broadcast on Nov 18.

Nov 8   A third recording for US television, for the teenage magazine programme *Boss City*. It is broadcast 3 days later on Nov 11.

Nov 11   Final concert of the US tour, at Winterland Auditorium, San Francisco.

Nov 14   Start of U.K. tour supporting the Jimi Hendrix Experience. Davey O'List of The Nice (also on the tour) is asked to stand in on occasion when Syd doesn't show up for the performance or cannot play.

Dec 5   The last concert on the Hendrix tour, at Green's Playhouse in Glasgow.

Dec 22   Christmas On Earth Continued is staged at Olympia in London. Pink Floyd are now advertising for an 'additional' guitarist, and Syd's old college friend, David Gilmour, is selected to join them.

1968

Jan   David Gilmour rehearses with Pink Floyd for the first time.

Jan 12   Pink Floyd appear as a five-member band for the first time, with both David Gilmour and Syd Barrett.

Jan 20   Syd Barrett appears live for the final time with Pink Floyd at a concert at Hastings.

Feb 17   Start of a short tour of The Netherlands and Belgium, which includes two sessions in Paris for French television. The tour finishes on Feb 25.

Mar   A statement is issued to the Press announcing that Syd Barrett has left the band. He is still signed to the same management company as a solo artiste.

Mar 5   Recording begins at EMI Studios in Abbey Road for the new single, "It Would Be So Nice".

Mar 28   The BBC film Pink Floyd performing for a forthcoming *Omnibus* special, "All My Loving", which is broadcast on Nov 3.

Apr 4   Pink Floyd begins four days of recording in London for the soundtrack of the movie *The Committee*, directed by Peter Sykes.

May 6   The First European International Pop Festival takes place in Italy, and Pink Floyd appear. Parts of the event are later broadcast on Italian and Dutch radio, and on German and British television.

May 11   Pink Floyd play a concert at the University of Sussex as part of the Brighton Arts Festival.

May 26   The band play at one of a series of concerts to benefit *Oz* magazine, at Middle Earth in Covent Garden, London.

May 31   Start of a short tour around Belgium and The Netherlands, which finishes on Jun 3.

Jun 28   The second Pink Floyd album, *A Saucerful Of Secrets*, is released, and the band performs it live for BBC's *Release*, a music magazine programme.

Jun 29   Pink Floyd appear at the first Hyde Park free concert, along with Jethro Tull and Tyrannosaurus Rex. After seeing them perform, influential music journalist John Peel becomes a major champion of their work.

Jul 8 Start of a North American tour, with a concert in Chicago. The tour continues until Aug 24 and includes an appearance at the Philadelphia Music Festival on Jul 24.

Oct 8 Start of recording sessions at EMI Studios in Abbey Road for "Point Me At The Sky".

Dec 2 Pink Floyd record two live shows, which are later broadcast on BBC Radio One.

Dec 28 A two-day festival is held in The Netherlands, and Pink Floyd are drafted in to replace Jimi Hendrix.

1969

Jan Start of recording sessions at EMI Studios in Abbey Road for the next album, *Ummagumma*.

Jan/Feb Studio sessions for the soundtrack of the movie *More*.

Apr 14 Pink Floyd perform a concert at the Royal Festival Hall *The Massed Gadgets Of Auximenes More Furious Madness From Pink Floyd*. The show featured two new pieces of music, *The Man* and *The Journey*.

Apr 27 The band's performance at Mothers, a club in Birmingham, is recorded for the album *Ummagumma*.

May 2 A performance at the Student Union in the College of Commerce in Manchester is recorded for the album *Ummagumma*.

May 9 Pink Floyd appear at the Camden Fringe Festival Free Concert on Hampstead Heath, London.

May 10 Nottingham's Pop & Blues Festival features Pink Floyd, along with Fleetwood Mac, The Tremeloes and Status Quo.

May 16 Opening night of a tour around England and Northern Ireland, with a concert in Leeds.

Jun 26 The UK tour finishes in London at the Royal Albert Hall with a show that culminates in the detonation of a large smoke bomb, which leads to Pink Floyd being banned from the venue for life.

Jul 4 Pink Floyd are the main attraction at an open-air concert staged as part of the Selby Arts Festival.

Jul 20 BBC television broadcasts an *Omnibus* special covering the landing of Apollo 11 on the moon, which features Pink Floyd in a live improvised performance.

Aug 8 The 9th National Jazz Pop Ballads & Blues Festival is held at Plumpton Racetrack in Sussex, and Pink Floyd are one of many bands that appear.

Nov 15 Syd Barrett releases his first and only solo single, "Octopus".

Dec Recording sessions at EMI Studios in Abbey Road for the soundtrack of *Zabriskie Point*.

1970

Jan 3 Syd Barrett's first solo album, *The Madcap Laughs* is released. He released one more album, *Barrett*, in November, after which he began to drop away from the music scene.

Jan/Feb A series of concerts is performed across England and France.

Mar Recording sessions begin for the new album, *Atom Heart Mother*, at EMI Studios in Abbey Road.

Mar 11 First concert in a European tour, at Offenbach in West Germany. The tour covers venues in West Germany, Sweden and Denmark, and culminates in an appearance at a music festival in France.

Apr 9 A US tour begins, with a concert in Manhattan. The tour is scheduled to finish in Dallas on May 23, but the final two dates are cancelled after all the band's equipment is stolen after the concert in New Orleans on May 16.

Jun 27 Pink Floyd appear at the Bath Festival of Blues & Progressive Music '70, along with most of the world's top music artistes.

Jun 28   The following day, the band make an appearance at the Holland Pop Festival, the largest popular music event in The Netherlands.

Jul 18   At the Hyde Park Free Concert, Pink Floyd play to thousands of people in London's Hyde Park.

Jul/Aug   The band moves to St Tropez in the South of France for the summer, partly on vacation and partly to appear at a series of planned music festivals in the area. In the event, many of the concerts are cancelled.

Sep 26   Start of a North American tour, with a concert in Philadelphia. The tour covered seven US states, but also included six venues in Canada. It finished in Boston on Oct 25.

Oct   Billboards on Sunset Strip are adorned with 40 foot high pictures of Lullubelle III, the cow featured on the cover of *Atom Heart Mother*, to publicize the album's release.

Nov 6   Start of a European tour with a concert in Amsterdam. The tour covers venues in The Netherlands, Sweden, Denmark, West Germany, and Switzerland, and finishes with a concert in Munich on Nov 29.

Dec 11   Start of a short tour of the UK with a concert in Brighton. It finishes with a concert in Manchester on Dec 22.

1971

Jan 4   Recording sessions begin at EMI Studios in Abbey Road for the next album, *Meddle*.

Feb 22   Start of a European tour with a concert in Lyon, which is cancelled at the last minute after violence breaks out at a Rolling Stones concert. The tour goes on to cover venues across West Germany, ending in a recording session for French television in Paris on Feb 27.

May 15   Pink Floyd top the bill at the Garden Party, a music festival at Crystal Palace in London.

Jun 4   Start of another European tour with a concert in Düsseldorf. The tour covers venues in West Germany, France, and Italy, ending in concert in Rome on Jun 20.

Aug 6   Start of a Japanese tour with a concert in Hakone, Japan. The tour goes on to Osaka in Japan, then over to Melbourne in Australia. It finishes with a concert in Sydney on Aug 15.

Sep 30   Pink Floyd record in front of a live audience for BBC television's *Sounds of the Seventies*, which is broadcast for the first time on Oct 12.

Oct 4–7   A film is made of Pink Floyd playing in the Roman Amphitheatre at Pompeii, which is later released as *Pink Floyd Live At Pompeii*.

Oct 15   A new North American tour opens with a concert in San Francisco. It goes on to cover 10 states across the US and three venues in Canada, finishing in Ohio on Nov 20.

1972

Jan 2   Syd Barrett plays at King's College Cellar, Cambridge with Twink and Eddie "Guitar" Burns; the group call themselves Stars. After only a couple more appearances they disband.

Jan/Feb   Recording begins at EMI Studios in Abbey Road for a new Pink Floyd album, *The Dark Side of the Moon*.

Jan 20   The first date on a new UK tour, at The Dome in Brighton. This was scheduled to be the first performance of *The Dark Side of The Moon* – later renamed *Eclipse* and then returning to its original name – but the band has to stop when only partway through and move onto other material after technical problems arise.

Jan 21   The UK tour continues with a concert in Portsmouth and moves around the UK, finishing in London on Feb 20.

Feb   Recording at Chateau d'Hérouville

23–29   outside Paris for the soundtrack of *La Vallée* (*The Valley*), which is later released as the album *Obscured By Clouds*.

Mar 6   First date on a Japanese tour, with a concert in Tokyo. It covers three more venues in Japan, finishing in Sapporo on Mar 13.

Mar 23–27   Final recording sessions at Chateau d'Hérouville to complete the album *Obscured By Clouds*.

Apr 14   A new Pink Floyd tour of the US begins with a concert in Tampa, Florida. It covers 11 states, finishing in Boston, Massachusetts, on May 4.

Sep 2   *Pink Floyd Live At Pompeii* receives its première at the Edinburgh Film Festival.

Sep 8   A North American tour begins with a concert in Austin, Texas. It covers seven states, and there are also three concerts in Canada. The final concert of the tour is played in Vancouver on Sep 30.

Oct 21   Pink Floyd play at a benefit concert at Wembley, on behalf of War On Want, The Albany Trust and Save The Children.

Nov 10/11   A new European tour begins with two concerts in Copenhagen, Denmark. The tour goes on to cover venues in West Germany, France, Belgium, and Switzerland.

Nov   Pink Floyd take time out of the European tour to rehearse and then perform the music for a Roland Petit ballet in Marseilles.

Dec 10   The European tour finishes with a concert in Lyon, France.

1973

Jan/Feb   Recording continues at EMI Studios in Abbey Road for the album *The Dark Side Of The Moon*.

Jan   Pink Floyd perform the music for eight performances of the Roland Petit ballet in Paris, but a further eight performances have to rely on a recorded playback as the band have other commitments.

Mar 4   Start of a North American tour with a concert in Madison, Wisconsin. The tour goes on to cover 12 more states and there are also two dates in Canada. It finishes in Atlanta, Georgia, on Mar 24.

May 18/19   At a concert at Earl's Court, London, *The Dark Side Of The Moon* is performed live.

Mar 28   *The Dark Side Of The Moon* becomes the first Pink Floyd album to hit No. 1 in the *Billboard* album chart.

Jun 17   Start of a US tour with a concert in Saratoga Springs, New York. The tour goes on to cover 8 more states and finishes in Tampa, Florida, on Jun 29.

Oct/Nov   Recording sessions at EMI Studios in Abbey Road for the *Household Objects* album, which is later abandoned after only a few tracks have been laid down.

Nov 4   Pink Floyd play a benefit concert

for recently disabled drummer Robert Wyatt, at the Rainbow Theatre in London.

1974

Jan   Start of recording sessions at EMI Studios in Abbey Road for the new album, *Wish You Were Here*.

Jun 18   Start of a short French tour with a concert in Toulouse. Concerts are also played in Poitiers, Dijon and Colmar, with a final series of three concerts in Paris from Jun 24–26.

Nov 4   Start of a short tour around the UK, with a concert in Edinburgh. The tour visits Newcastle, London, Stoke-On-Trent, Cardiff, Liverpool, Birmingham, and Manchester and finishes with two concerts in Bristol on Dec 13–14.

1975

Jan   Sessions continue at EMI Studios in Abbey Road for *Wish You Were Here*.

Apr 8   Start of a short North American tour with a concert in Vancouver, Canada. It also covers five states in the U.S, finishing in Los Angeles, California on Apr 27.

May/Jun   Sessions continue at EMI Studios in Abbey Road for *Wish You Were Here*. During one of the final sessions, Syd Barrett turns up at the studio but is initially not recognized due to his changed appearance.

Jun 7   Start of a new North American tour with a concert in Atlanta, Georgia. It covers seven other states in the U.S, finishing with two concerts in Canada on Jun 26 (Quebec) and Jun 28 (Ontario).

Jul 5   At the Knebworth Park festival, Pink Floyd première new material from *Wish You Were Here*.

1976

Apr/Dec Recording sessions at Pink Floyd's own studio in Islington, North London for the next album, *Animals*.

Apr   David Gilmour's house is broken into. Thieves take guitars valued at UK£ 7,000.

Aug 2   Peter "Puddy" Watts, road manager and one of the voices on "The Dark Side Of The Moon", dies of a heroin overdose.

Dec 2/3 Hipgnosis photo shoot for the *Animals* album cover at Battersea Power Station in London. On the second day the helium-filled inflatable pig that has been tethered at the location for the photograph breaks free and eventually comes to earth in a field in Kent.

1977

Jan 19   The Press launch for *Animals* is held at the Sports & Social Club at Battersea Power Station.

Jan 20   The album *Animals* is played from start to finish on air for the

first time during the *John Peel Show* on BBC Radio One.

Jan 23   First concert on an extensive European tour, at Dortmund in West Germany. The tour visits several venues in West Germany then heads off to Austria, Switzerland, The Netherlands, Belgium, and France. The final concert is held in Munich on Mar 1.

Mar 15   Pink Floyd play five concerts at Wembley, then two in Stafford in the UK.

Apr 22   A North American tour begins with a concert in Miami, Florida. The first half of the tour covers seven states; after a month-long break, the second half covers a further eight states and finishes in Montreal in Canada on Jul 6.

1978

Jan   David Gilmour and Richard Wright both work on their own solo albums in different studios in France.

May 26   *David Gilmour*, the guitarist's first solo album is released.

Sep 22   Richard Wright releases *Wet Dream*, his first solo album.

Sep–Dec Roger Waters works alone at the Pink Floyd's Islington studios to develop material for what will become *The Wall*, as well as for his first solo album, *The Pros and Cons of Hitchhiking*.

1979

Jan–Jul   Pink Floyd begin recording sessions for *The Wall* in studios in France.

Sep–Oct Recording for *The Wall* continues in Los Angeles and New York.

Oct   Richard Wright is asked to leave Pink Floyd during final sessions for *The Wall*, after his relationship with Roger Waters breaks down. However, he continues playing with the band for live performances as a paid session musician.

Nov 23   "Another Brick In The Wall Part 2" is released. It goes straight to No.1 in the U.K. charts – the band's only No.1 single.

1980

Feb 7–13 Pink Floyd play *The Wall* live at a series of seven concerts in Los Angeles, California. The show has to be halted for a short time after special effects fireworks set fire to some drapes.

Feb   The band play *The Wall* live
24–28   at a series of five concerts in Long Island, New York.

Mar 22   *The Dark Side Of The Moon* breaks the previous record for the longest stay on the Billboard Top 100 and goes on to remain there for a total of 741 weeks from 1973 to 1988, longer than any other album in history.

Aug 4–9 The band play *The Wall* live at a series of six concerts at Earl's Court in London. Ten original

Gerald Scarfe drawings for *The Wall*, worth more than UK£30,000, are stolen from the foyer of Earl's Court, including the original artwork for the cover of the album.

1981

Feb   Pink Floyd play *The Wall* live at a series of eight concerts in Dortmund, West Germany.

May 1   Nick Mason releases his first album, *Fictitious Sports*, made with Carla Bley and Robert Wyatt.

Jun 13–18   Pink Floyd play *The Wall* live at a series of six concerts at Earl's Court in London. It would be the last time that Roger Waters appeared in concert with the band for 24 years.

Sep   Start of filming at Pinewood Studios for the movie, *Pink Floyd The Wall*, directed by Alan Parker.

1982

May 23   The world première of *Pink Floyd The Wall* takes place at the Cannes Film Festival in the South of France.

Jul–Dec   Recording begins at Pink Floyd's studio in Islington for *The Final Cut*.

1983

Mar 23   Press reception in Manhattan to launch *The Final Cut* in the US

1984

Mar 5   David Gilmour releases his second solo album, *About Face*, which includes two songs

co-written with Pete Townshend.

Apr 9   Release of *Identity*, an album covering Richard Wright's collaboration with Dave Harris in the group Zee.

May 8   Roger Waters releases his first solo album, *The Pros And Cons Of Hitch Hiking*.

1985

Jul 13   David Gilmour appears at Live Aid as part of Bryan Ferry's band.

Aug 19   Nick Mason and ex-10cc guitarist Rick Fenn release their joint album, *Profiles*.

Oct   Roger Waters makes application to the High Court to prevent the Pink Floyd name being used further, as a way of ensuring that the group will cease to exist now that he no longer wishes to be a member. At around the same time, he invokes the 'leaving member' clause to end his contract with EMI and CBS.

1986

Oct   The case to resolve ownership of the Pink Floyd name comes to the High Court, but Roger Waters eventually drops his legal action and allows the others to continue as Pink Floyd.

Oct 27   Release of the soundtrack album to the movie *When The Wind Blows*, which features music written and performed by Roger Waters.

Nov/Dec   Recording sessions on Astoria, David Gilmour's houseboat studio on the river at Hampton, for the next Pink Floyd album, *A Momentary Lapse Of Reason*, with Gilmour and Nick Mason.

1987

Jan/Feb   Further recording sessions on Astoria for *A Momentary Lapse Of Reason*.

Feb/Mar   Further recording sessions at studios in Los Angeles for *A Momentary Lapse Of Reason*.

Jun 15   800 rented NHS beds are lined up on Saunton Sands in North Devon for Storm Thorgerson to shoot the cover for *A Momentary Lapse Of Reason*.

Jun 15   Roger Waters releases his second solo album, *Radio K.A.O.S.*

Sep 7   David Gilmour, Nick Mason and Richard Wright release *A Momentary Lapse Of Reason* as Pink Floyd.

Sep 9   First concert in the *A Momentary Lapse Of Reason* tour, held in Ontario, Canada. Originally scheduled for 11 weeks, it lasts over 22 months and covers North America, New Zealand, Australia, Japan, and Europe, finally coming to an end with a concert in Marseilles, France on Jul 18 1989.

Dec 23   David Gilmour and Roger Waters sign an agreement on the business affairs of Pink Floyd, although the bad feeling between them continues for some years to come.

1988

Jan/Feb The *A Momentary Lapse Of Reason* tour covers New Zealand and Australia.

Mar   The tour moves on to Japan for eight concerts in Japan.

Apr–Jun The tour goes back to North America for 28 concerts over 16 states plus two concerts in Canada

Jun–Aug The European leg of the tour travels to France, The Netherlands, West Germany, Austria, Italy, Spain, Switzerland Denmark, Norway, and England. The shows in Versailles, on Jun 21 and 22, are filmed for the *Delicate Sound Of Thunder* video.

Aug   Another leg of the *A Momentary Lapse Of Reason* tour consists of 10 concerts across three US states.

Oct 17   A collection of out-takes and unheard tracks by Syd Barrett made during the late sixties and early seventies is released under the title, *Opel*.

Nov 26   A copy of *Delicate Sound Of Thunder* travels into space to the Russian space station MIR.

1989

May–Jul The final leg of the *A Momentary Lapse Of Reason* tour begins on May 13 with a concert in Belgium and travels to Italy, England, Greece, Russia, Finland, Sweden, West Germany, Austria, France, and The Netherlands. The tour finally comes to an end with a concert in France on Jul 18.

Jul 15   Pink Floyd plays Venice on a floating stage, in a show that is broadcast live around the world and is seen by an estimated 100 million people.

1990

Jun 30   Pink Floyd are one of the supergroups to play Knebworth Festival in aid of Nordorf-Robbins Music Therapy Centre.

Jul 21   Roger Waters stages *The Wall – Live In Berlin* in Berlin's Potsdamerplatz with a variety of guest artistes on behalf of the Memorial Fund For Disaster Relief.

1992

Sep 7   Roger Waters releases his new solo album, *Amused To Death*.

1993

Jan–Dec Pink Floyd return to the studio in Islington and Chiswick to start recording *The Division Bell*.

Apr 26   EMI release *Crazy Diamond – The Complete Syd Barrett* as a box set.

Sep 18   Pink Floyd appear at the Cowdray Ruins Concert, a benefit in aid of the King Edward VII hospital in Midhurst.

1994

Jan 10   A Press reception in Weeksville, North Carolina to announce the new album and world tour features a specially painted airship, which travelled over many cities in the US over the next six months.

Mar 21   The UK Press reception features a second specially painted airship, which goes on to make a promotional tour around Europe.

Mar 30   The North/South American leg of The Division Bell tour kicks off with a concert in Miami, Florida. It covers 24 other US states, and there are also three concerts in Mexico and ten in Canada. The tour finishes with a concert in Rutherford, New Jersey, on Jul 18.

Jul 22   With a break of only a few days, the first concert of the European leg of The Division Bell tour is played in Lisbon, Portugal. The tour moves on to dates in Spain, France, Germany, Switzerland, Austria, Denmark, Sweden, Norway, Belgium, The Netherlands, Czech Republic, and Italy. The last concert is played in Lausanne, Switzerland, on Sep 25.

Aug 7 UK newspaper *The News Of The World* reports that celebrity accountant Martin Stainton has vanished, possibly with millions of pound of his clients' money. He was accountant for Richard Wright, and also Rod Stewart, Tina Turner, Bon Jovi and Simple Minds, amongst others.

Oct 12 The Division Bell tour moves to the UK, for a series of 14 performances at Earl's Court in London. The first concert, on Oct 12, has to be rescheduled to Oct 17 after a section of seating collapses and several people are injured.

Oct 29 Final concert of The Division Bell tour, at Earl's Court. It is estimated that in total the tour played to more that 5 million people in 68 cities.

1995
Jun 5 Release of *Pulse*, a double album covering The Division Bell tour. It is followed a week later by a video.

1996
Jan 17 Pink Floyd are inducted into the Rock And Roll Hall Of Fame in a ceremony in New York.

Nov 26 Release of Richard Wright's solo album, *Broken China*.

2000
Dec 4 Release of Roger Waters' solo album, *In The Flesh*.

2002
May 7 Release of Roger Waters' album of demo versions of earlier songs, *Flickering Flame*.

2004
Oct 7 Publication of Nick Mason's memoirs, *Inside Out – A Personal History of Pink Floyd*.

2005
Jul 2 Pink Floyd, including Richard Wright, are reunited with Roger Waters for a performance at Live 8 in London's Hyde Park. It is the first time the four have been on stage together for 24 years.

2006
Mar 6 UK release of David Gilmour's third solo album, *On An Island*. It is released in the US on the following day.

July 7 Syd Barrett dies at his home in Cambridgeshire aged 60.

Sep 26 Release of Roger Waters' album *Ça Ira*, an opera in three acts.

2007
Sep 17 Release of the DVD *Remember That Night? David Gilmour Live At The Albert Hall*.

2008
Sep 15 Richard Wright dies of cancer.

Sep 22 UK release of David Gilmour's fourth solo album, *Live in Gdansk*, a live recording of him performing during his 2006 tour

2010
July 10 Gilmour and Waters perform together at a charity event for the Hoping Foundation in Oxfordshire, UK.

2011
May 12 David Gilmour plays "Comfortably Numb" along with Roger Waters at one of Waters' performances of The Wall at the O2 Arena, London. Nick Mason and Gilmour then join Waters for "Outside The Wall".

Sept 26 EMI reissues the band's back catalogue in newly remastered versions

Discography

ALBUMS

1967

Aug 4 *The Piper at the Gates of Dawn* (UK only)

Oct 21 *Pink Floyd* (US only)

1968

Jun 28 *A Saucerful of Secrets* (US release date Jul 27)

1969

June 13 *More* (US release date Aug 9) – movie soundtrack

Nov 7 *Ummagumma* (US release date Nov 8)

1970

Oct 2 *Atom Heart Mother* (US release date Oct 10)

1971

May 14 *Relics* (US release date Jul 17)

Oct 30 *Meddle* (UK release date Nov 5)

1972

Jun 2 *Obscured by Clouds* (US release date Jun 17) – based on the movie soundtrack for *La Vallée* (*The Valley*)

1973

Mar 10 *The Dark Side Of The Moon* (UK release date Mar 23)

1974

Jan 18 *A Nice Pair* (US release date Dec 8) – re-release of the first two albums

1975

Apr *Tour '75* (US only) – promotional album

Sep 12 *Wish You Were Here* (US release date Sep 13)

1977

Jan 21 *Animals* (US release date Feb 12)

1979

Jul 6 *Pink Floyd First XI* (UK only) – limited edition

Nov 30 *The Wall* (US release date Dec 8)

1980

Dec *Pink Floyd – Off The Wall* (US only) – promotional album

1981

Nov 23 *A Collection Of Great Dance Songs*

1983

Mar 21 *The Final Cut* (US release date Apr 2)

June 18 *Works* (US only)

1987

Sep 7 *A Momentary Lapse Of Reason* (US release date Sep 8)

1988

Jun *Pink Floyd In Europe* (UK only) – promotional EP

Nov 22 *Delicate Sound of Thunder*

1990

Sep 17 *The Wall Live In Berlin*

1992

Nov 2 *Shine On* – CD box set

Nov *A CD Full Of Secrets* (US only) – promotional CD

1993

Mar 24 *The Dark Side Of The Moon* – 20th Anniversary edition

Apr 5 *Pink Floyd Gift Set* (US only)

1994

Mar 28 *The Division Bell* (US release date Apr 5)

1995

Jun 5 *Pulse*

1997

Aug 4 *The Piper At The Gates Of Dawn* – 30th Anniversary mono edition

Aug 18 *1997 Vinyl Collection* (UK only) – LP box set)

2000

Mar 27 *Is There Anybody Out There? The Wall Live: Pink Floyd 1980–81* (US limited edition release date Apr 17)

Sep *Wish You Were Here* – 25th Anniversary edition

2001

Nov 5 *Echoes – The Best of Pink Floyd*

2003

Mar 31 *The Dark Side Of The Moon* – 30th Anniversary edition

2004

Mar 29 *The Final Cut* – re-release including "When The Tigers Broke Free"

2007

Sep 3 *The Piper At The Gates Of Dawn* – 40th Anniversary edition

Dec 10 *Oh By The Way* – box set

2008

Jan 13 *Wish You Were Here* – remastered edition

VIDEOS & DVDs

1972

Sep 2 *Pink Floyd Live At Pompeii* – VHS

1982

May 23 *Pink Floyd The Wall* – VHS

1983
Apr 25   *The Final Cut* – (UK only) VHS

1989
Jun 12   *Delicate Sound Of Thunder* –VHS

1995
Jun 12   *Pulse, Earls Court London* – VHS
Oct 2   *Pink Floyd London 66–67* – VHS

2003
Mar 24   *The Pink Floyd & Syd Barrett Story* – DVD
Aug 26   *Classic Albums – The Making Of The Dark Side Of The Moon* (UK only) – VHS

2005
Nov 7   *Live 8* – DVD

2006
July 10   *Pulse* – DVD

2008
Oct 6   *Pink Floyd – The Great Gig In The Sky* – DVD box set
Oct 28   *A Technicolor Dream* (US only) – DVD

SINGLES
1967
Mar 10   "Arnold Layne"/"Candy And A Currant Bun" (US release date Apr 24)
Jun 16   "See Emily Play"/"Scarecrow"

(US release date Jul 24)
Nov 6   "Flaming"/"The Gnome" (US only)
Nov 18   "Apples And Oranges"/"Paintbox" (UK only)

1968
Apr 19   "It Would Be So Nice"/"Julia Dream" (US release date Jun 3)
Aug 19   "Let There Be More Light"/"Remember A Day" (US only)
        "Point Me At The Sky"/"Careful With That Axe, Eugene" (UK only)

1971
Nov 29   "One of These Days"/"Fearless"

1972
Jul 10   "Free Four"/"The Gold It's In The..."

1973
May 7   "Money"/"Any Colour You Like"
Oct   "Time"/"Breathe"/"Us And Them"/"Money" (EP, US only)

1974
Feb 4   "Time"/"Us And Them" (US only)

1975
Nov   "Have A Cigar"/"Welcome To The Machine" (US only)

"Have A Cigar"/"Shine On You Crazy Diamond Parts I-V" (Italy & France only)

1979
Nov 23   "Another Brick in The Wall Part 2"/"One of My Turns" (US release Jan 7, 1980)

1980
Jun 9   "Run Like Hell"/"Don't Leave Me Now"
Jun 23   "Comfortably Numb"/"Hey You"

1982
Jul 26   "When The Tigers Broke Free"/"Bring The Boys Back Home"

1983
May 3   "Not Now John"/"The Hero's Return Part 1 & 2"

1987
Aug   "Learning To Fly"/"One Slip"/"Terminal Frost"/"Terminal Frost"
Dec   "On The Turning Away"/"Run Like Hell"

1988
Jun 13   "One Slip"/"Terminal Frost"

1994
May 16   "Take It Back"/"Astronomy Domine"/"Take It

Back"
Jul   "High Hopes"/"Marooned"
Dec 17   "High Hopes"/"Keep Talking"/"One Of These Days"

1995
        "Wish You Were Here"/"Coming Back To Life"/"Keep Talking"

1997
        1967 The First Three Singles

2000
Oct   "Money"/"Time" (US only)
        "Wish You Were Here"/"Have A Cigar"

Acknowledgements

Thanks to Alice Hill, Cliff Salter, Hayley Newman, Rick Mayston, Wendy Toole,
Sarah Rickayzen and Anthony McAndrew.

Picture Credits
The photographs in this book and front cover image are © Getty Images except the following:
© Corbis: Pages 18, 42, 91, 92, 93, 114, 115, 116, 117, 138, 140, 142, 152, 171
King Collection/Retna 46   DISTER Alain [Dister/DALLE] /Retna   49   Peter Mazel / Sunshine /
Retna 62, 63, 64, 65, 66, 67, 68, 69, 95, 107, 108, 109, 118   Gysbert Hanekroot /Sunshine /Retna
70, 71, 88, 124, 125, 126, 127
Tolca / Sunshine / Retna 106
© Atlantic Publishing: Pages 26, 27 and back cover